Student Dress Codes and the First Amendment

Student Dress Codes and the First Amendment

Legal Challenges and Policy Issues

Richard Fossey and Todd A. DeMitchell

ROWMAN & LITTLEFIELD
Lanham • Boulder • New York • London

Published by Rowman & Littlefield
A wholly owned subsidiary of The Rowman & Littlefield Publishing Group, Inc.
4501 Forbes Boulevard, Suite 200, Lanham, Maryland 20706
www.rowman.com

16 Carlisle Street, London W1D 3BT, United Kingdom

British Library Cataloguing in Publication Information Available

Library of Congress Cataloging-in-Publication Data Available

978-1-4758-0203-0 (cloth : alk. paper)
978-1-4758-0204-7 (pbk.   )
978-1-4758-0205-4 (electronic)

Printed in the United States of America

It is worth remembering that, whether this decision is correct or not, no other court system in the world today, and none that has existed in the history of the world, would take so much time to address the concerns of two high school students sent home over their T-shirts. Whatever the outcome, claims of violation of free expression are given the greatest attention, even when they arise in miniature, by this country, this judicial system and this court.

Pyle v. South Hadley School Committee (1993)

Contents

Preface

tinker v. Desmoines [handwritten annotation]

The medium is the message.

—Marshall McLuhan[1]

What are students thinking about in the morning as they choose the clothes they will wear to school for the day? Do they want to wear something fashionable or something they think will make them more attractive to the opposite sex? Do they choose clothing that will boost their confidence, or are they simply looking for something to wear that is reasonably clean?

Based on our review of federal court decisions, it is clear that some students choose their school clothing to make some sort of statement. They may wish to express their views on a political or social issue, their attitudes about authority, their affinity for a sports team, or their religious beliefs. Often they express their views on that ubiquitous item of student clothing—the T-shirt.

Since time immemorial, schools have enforced student dress codes, which put restrictions on what students may wear to school. In general, schools adopt student dress codes in order to maintain an educational environment that facilitates instruction and orderliness. Although the details of these codes vary widely, they generally articulate standards of modesty, cleanliness, and decorum. A code might dictate standards for girls' skirt length, for example, or require boys to keep their shirttails tucked in their pants. Student dress codes usually forbid bawdy messages on clothing, messages that promote the use of illegal drugs, or expressions that demean other students.

From time to time, students have challenged school dress codes in court, arguing that the messages proclaimed on their clothing are constitutionally protected under the First Amendment. Indeed, in *Tinker v. Des Moines Independent Community School District*, the Supreme Court ruled more than forty years ago that students have a constitutional right to freedom of expression while they are in the school environment.[2] And numerous lower court decisions have ruled that this constitutional right of expression may include the messages that students proclaim on their clothing.

Nevertheless, in the years since the *Tinker* case was decided, the Supreme Court has made clear that a student's right to free expression is not unlimited when the student is at school. As Chief Justice Burger stated in *Bethel School District No. 403 v. Fraser*, "the constitutional rights of stu-

[handwritten margin notes: "public schools + real world so is right + rw rights"]

dents in public school are not automatically coextensive with the rights of adults in other settings."[3] Rather, as one federal court asserted, a public school student's right to free speech must be "balanced against the need to foster an educational atmosphere free from undue disruptions to appropriate discipline."[4]

[handwritten margin note: "sup court decisions"]

Over the years, the Supreme Court has sketched out some of the limits on students' constitutional right to freedom of expression while they are in the school environment. In the *Bethel* case, the Court held that schools have the authority to censor student speech that is vulgar, lewd, or profane. In *Hazelwood School District v. Kuhlmeier*, the Court stated that schools can regulate student speech that is school-sponsored.[5] And in *Morse v. Frederick*, the Supreme Court upheld the right of school authorities to ban student expression that promotes or celebrates the use of illegal drugs.[6]

These Supreme Court decisions have helped school administrators understand the limits of their constitutional authority when they seek to regulate student speech, including speech on students' clothing; but disputes continue to arise between students and school officials regarding what students wear to school. Again and again, the federal courts have been called on to determine whether a student has a First Amendment right to wear a particular item of clothing that school officials seek to ban as being in violation of their school's student dress code.

Thus, educators are required to balance two sometimes conflicting responsibilities: On the one hand they are charged with providing high-quality education in a safe and non-abusive environment. On the other hand, they are required to respect their students' constitutional right to freedom of expression, which they sometimes exercise by proclaiming messages on their clothing.

Often the schools win these cases. In *Gano v. School District No. 411*, for example, a federal district judge upheld the suspension of a student who wore a T-shirt showing three school administrators inebriated.[7] And in *Baxter v. Vigo County School Corporation*, the suspension of a Lost Creek Elementary school student for wearing T-shirts that read "Unfair Grades," "Racism," and "I Hate Lost Creek" was upheld.[8]

On the other hand, students regularly win some of these cases. For example, a federal court in Pennsylvania ruled that students have the constitutional right to wear bracelets that proclaimed, "I ♥ Boobies" to show their support for breast cancer awareness.[9] And the Seventh Circuit Court of Appeals ruled that school officials could not prohibit students from wearing T-shirts to school that proclaimed "Be Happy, Not Gay."[10]

Dress codes sit at that intersection of students' constitutional right to free speech and the compelling need for the public schools to establish and maintain a suitable environment for education.[11] We will explore this intersection throughout the book.

We have studied and implemented dress codes from two different perspectives and one shared perspective. Richard practiced school law in Alaska and helped school districts craft dress codes that protected school environments while striving to respect students' legitimate right to engage in free speech. Todd was an elementary school teacher, a principal (K–8), and school superintendent (K–8) in California, where he implemented and enforced dress codes. As legal researchers, we have studied student dress codes for over fifteen years and analyzed the many federal court decisions regarding the constitutional limitations on these codes. The legal aspects of student attire is a subject that we have often written about in the scholarly literature, and we hope our readers will find our perspectives and analysis helpful.

- two male authors
- white ?

ORGANIZATION OF THE BOOK

This book focuses on legal and policy issues pertaining to student dress codes and is organized into six chapters. The first chapter sets the stage for the rest of the book by discussing the controversy about student expression through clothing choices and the challenges that confront public school educators who seek to respect the constitutional rights of their students while enforcing policies designed to ensure the efficient delivery of educational services and the protection of a proper learning environment for students.

Chapter 2 examines the four United States Supreme Court decisions on the constitutional rights of students to engage in free speech while at school: *Tinker v. Des Moines Independent School District*,[12] *Bethel School District No. 403 v. Fraser*,[13] *Hazelwood School District v. Kuhlmeier*,[14] and *Morse v. Frederick*.[15]

This chapter also discusses three important First Amendment cases decided by the Supreme Court outside the school context: *United States v. O'Brien*,[16] *Spence v. Washington*,[17] and *Texas v. Johnson*.[18] Although none of these decisions involve student speech in the school environment, the lower federal courts have occasionally looked to these three opinions when deciding constitutional disputes about student attire.

The following three chapters explore discrete categories of student dress code litigation. Chapter 3 examines cases involving nonspecific messages on student clothing, such as *Bivens v. Albuquerque Public Schools*, in which a student claimed a constitutional right to wear sagging pants to school.[19] Chapter 4, entitled "Drugs, Politics, and the Confederate Battle Flag: Targeted Messages on Students' Clothing," is an analysis of the extensive litigation involving political messages, drugs, and the Confederate flag. Chapter 5 continues our review of content-specific messages involving student attire. It surveys lawsuits concerning abortion, sex, and sexual orientation.

In the sixth chapter, we offer some recommendations to school authorities regarding how to draft student dress codes that will pass constitutional muster under the First Amendment. In addition, we attempt to bring the policy implications of dress code policies into focus.

In this concluding chapter, we argue for a balance between the rights of students to express themselves at school and the responsibilities of educators to maintain a safe, orderly, and respectful school environment. We question whether the public schools should be forced to defend their decisions about what students wear to school in the federal courts. Defending a lawsuit can be expensive, and surely money spent litigating in federal court would be better spent educating students.

We also question whether parents are sending their children the right message about civic rights and responsibilities when they argue in federal courts that their children have a constitutionally protected right to wear a particular item of clothing to school. And finally, we question whether the federal courts are serving the best interests of schools, students, or society at large by giving serious attention to students who come to court arguing they have a constitutional right to attend school wearing whatever they choose to wear. After all, students have adequate venues for expressing their views while at school in student clubs, school newspapers, and appropriate forums for student discussions and debates. We do not see the wisdom or constitutional necessity of turning the scarce resources of the federal judiciary to the examination of school regulations about student attire.

NOTES

1. Marshall McLuhan, *Understanding Media: The Extensions of Man* (New York: New American Library, 1964), 1. "This is merely to say that the personal and social consequences of any medium—that is, of any extension of ourselves—result from the new scale that is introduced into our affairs by each extension of ourselves, or by any new technology." Ibid.

2. Tinker v. Des Moines Independent Community School District, 393 U.S. 503 (1969).

3. Bethel School District No. 403 v. Fraser, 478 U.S. 675, 682 (1986).

4. Bivens v. Albuquerque Public Schools, 889 F. Supp. 556, 559 (D.N.M. 1995).

5. Hazelwood School District v. Kuhlmeier, 484 U.S. 260 (1989).

6. Morse v. Frederick, 551 U.S. 393 (2007).

7. Gano v. School District No. 411, 674 F. Supp. 796 (D. Idaho 1987).

8. Baxter v. Vigo County School Corporation, 26 F.3d 728 (7th Cir. 1994).

9. B.H. v. Easton Area School District, 725 F.3d 293 (3d Cir. 2013).

10. Nuxoll v. Indian Prairie School District, 523 F.3d 668 (7th Cir. 2008).

11. The Supreme Court has recognized that schools have a "compelling interest in having an undisputed school session conducive to the students' learning" (Grayned v. City of Rockford, 408 U.S. 104, 119 [1972]).

12. 393 U.S. 503 (1969).

13. 478 U.S. 675 (1986).

14. 484 U.S. 260 (1989).

15. 551 U.S. 393 (2007).

16. 391 U.S. 367 (1968).
17. 418 U.S. 405 (1974).
18. 491 U.S. 397 (1989).
19. Bivens v. Albuquerque Public Schools, 889 F. Supp. 556, 559 (D.N.M. 1995).

ONE

What to Wear to School

The Controversy

When asked about the need for student dress codes, a principal from a rural area responded, "Some would come Nude without it."[1]

The Anderson County School District in Tennessee, like many school districts throughout the nation, adopted a student code of conduct that included regulations on student dress. The dress code stated that student attire "or appearance, which tends to draw attention to an individual rather than to a learning situation, must be avoided."[2] The code banned clothing and accessories that displayed racial or ethnic slurs, gang affiliations, vulgar or suggestive language or images, and promotions of products that students are not legally entitled to purchase or possess such as alcohol, illegal drugs, and tobacco.[3]

School authorities claimed that racial tension had existed at the district's Clinton High School dating back to 1956, when the school was first integrated. For that reason, the school banned the Confederate flag, which school officials said "would be a distraction to any student offended by it and could result in some sort of dangerous disagreement resulting from conflict or violence."[4] ← reason for banning flag

On October 30, 2006, Tom Defoe, a student, wore a T-shirt that depicted the image of the Confederate flag. When school officials asked him to remove the T-shirt or to turn it inside out, he refused. He was sent home. Six days later, he wore a belt buckle to school with a Confederate flag displayed on it. He was subsequently suspended from school.[5]

On November 20, 2006, Tom Defoe, with his parents, sued the school district for a violation of Tom's free speech rights. A weeklong jury trial was conducted during the summer of 2008. The jury was unable to reach a unanimous verdict. The federal district court judge granted summary

be wanted flag garb ← now

1

judgment for the defendant school district.[6] The plaintiff student and his parents appealed to the Sixth Circuit Court of Appeals.

On appeal, a three-judge panel affirmed the trial court's decision in favor of the school district. In a concurring opinion, one judge acknowledged that the Confederate flag is subject to various interpretations. On the one hand, the battle flag is seen by some as conveying "a noble message," signifying "honor for one's ancestors who fought bravely . . . for independence from the industrialized North."[7] But on the other hand, the Confederate flag "is doubtless *perceived* by many, if not most, student viewers in today's high schools in the United States as a statement of racial hostility—comparable to a slogan that says 'Blacks should be slaves' or 'Blacks are inferior.'"[8]

Certainly, in the concurring judge's opinion, "[a] plainly reasonable interpretation of a Confederate flag T-shirt or jacket is one of racial hostility or contempt, regardless of the subjective intent of the wearer."[9] And even if a student displayed a Confederate flag without intending to communicate racial hostility, "a school administrator cannot practically administer a rule that permits such clothing sometimes and prohibits it other times, depending on the intent of each individual wearer."[10]

The *Defoe* case illustrates the challenges that educators face as they attempt to honor the free speech rights of students while maintaining a safe and orderly educational atmosphere. Unfortunately, in recent years, public school districts are increasingly being sued by students and their parents based on claims that school authorities violated a student's free speech rights under the First Amendment by enforcing a student dress code that restricted a student's choice of clothing.

These controversies are costly to school districts and taxpayers. For example, in a 2008 case, a student sued her school district on First Amendment grounds after school authorities banned her from wearing or displaying slogans advocating the fair treatment of gay and lesbian students. The student won her suit, which resulted in a judgment of one dollar against the school district, obviously a trivial amount. Attorney's fees, however, and other litigation expenses cost the school district $325,000.[11] These are not inconsequential costs for an educator's disciplinary decision.

When defending their student dress codes in court, most school districts do not attempt to justify their dress codes based on research or policy arguments that such policies improve student achievement. Rather, school districts generally justify their dress codes on the grounds that such codes prevent disruptions caused by certain types of clothing and support the learning environment. They argue that dress codes help students focus on learning by banning provocative clothing and advertisements for illegal behavior such as drug use or alcohol consumption.

The arguments for not allowing students to wear certain advertisements or banning clothing that is too revealing are not aimed at improving attendance, achieving better results on standardized tests, or developing community spirit. Rather, school authorities adopt dress codes with the simple goal of creating a purposeful learning environment that reflects community values. Dress-code advocates do not assert that banning sagging pants (precariously worn to reveal colorful boxers), crop-top T-shirts, or torn jeans will result in anything more than a more businesslike environment for students and adults.

Thus, the policy objectives of a student dress code and the rationale for adopting a school uniform code are different. Schools adopt dress codes simply to maintain a disciplined learning environment, while schools that introduce student-uniform codes often do so with the specific goal of enhancing student achievement. Indeed the policy objectives for student dress codes are different enough from the policy goals for school uniform policies that the two types of regulations are discussed in separate volumes. In this volume, we confine ourselves to a discussion of school dress codes that have been litigated in the courts. In our second volume, we examine what the research says about the benefits of student uniforms as a means of improving student achievement and the constitutionality of school regulations that require students to wear specified uniforms while they are in school.

THE BALANCING ACT

For many students, what to wear to school is an innocuous question that is often answered by locating something in the closet that is clean (or reasonably clean). For other students the decision about what to wear to school involves the student's personal beliefs and values and is linked to the student's nascent development of self and personal values. For example, Aloysius Dreaming Bear brought a lawsuit against his school district, hoping to win the right to wear his traditional Lakota clothing to his high school graduation instead of the required cap and gown.[12]

School officials and students do not always share the same opinion of what is appropriate to wear to school. But if a school chooses to adopt a specific policy that restricts what students may wear to school, that policy must comport with established and guaranteed constitutional freedoms.

There are legitimate reasons for schools to adopt student dress codes. Some of these reasons involve safety (chains, spiked collars, and flip flops). Schools have a legitimate concern, for example, about students wearing loose clothing around machinery commonly found in industrial arts classes.

Other concerns involve the impressionable age of the students and the inappropriateness of certain types of dress (revealing clothes, clothes that advertise drugs and alcohol). One high school in New Hampshire expressed its desire for modesty by developing a student dress code around what school officials called the "4 Bs" —bellies, butts, breasts, and box-ers.[13] You can have them; you just can't show them.

And some school officials adopt dress codes to prohibit clothes that can cause disruptions, interfere with the school mission, or glorify gangs. Many schools have policies that prohibit students from wearing clothing that celebrate the illegal use of drugs or alcohol, and some have codes that prohibit students from wearing clothing associated with gang activity.

Community standards have influenced several dress code cases. In 1987, students sued an Ohio school district for refusing to allow them to attend a prom dressed as a person of the opposite sex.[14] A federal court found no First Amendment violation, however. In the court's view, schools have the authority to enforce dress regulations that teach community values and promote school discipline.

The same year, an Illinois student challenged a school rule, invoked to curtail gang activity, against males wearing earrings.[15] Like the Ohio cross-dressers, the plaintiff lost this case. However, community standards change. Unlike the Ohio cross-dressing students, a female student brought suit when she was denied the opportunity to attend her prom with her girlfriend wearing a tuxedo. The federal district court found that the student's free speech rights were abridged, asserting that the "expression and communication of her viewpoint is the type of speech that falls squarely within the purview of the First Amendment."[16]

One legal commentator has asserted that the "'[t]he Achilles' Heel' of dress codes is the difficulty in defining what is proper attire in the classroom without violating the basic constitutional rights of students."[17] While public school students enjoy some degree of freedom of speech within the schoolhouse gates, the courts have recognized that this freedom must be balanced against the need to foster an educational atmosphere free from undue disruptions. Moreover, although some student clothing clearly conveys a particular message—T-shirts proclaiming political messages, for example—not all clothing choices have enough expressive content to be protected by the Free Speech clause of the First Amendment

For example, in a New Mexico case involving a student's asserted constitutional right to wear "sagging pants," a federal judge concluded that most people would not interpret the wearing of droopy pants as conveying a message. Moreover, the judge noted, the "communication of ideas must be measured against substantial and compelling societal goals such as safety, decency, individual rights of other citizens, and the smooth functioning of government."[18]

Thus, while students possess free speech rights, those rights can sometimes be somewhat abridged within the special environment of the public school; and those rights must be balanced against the legitimate interests of school authorities. This book explores the contours of that legal balance as articulated by the federal courts.

Without a doubt, considerable litigation has established that the once benign and mundane issue of what students choose to wear to school is now draped with constitutional considerations. The constitutionality of student dress codes has been litigated in federal courts all over the United States. This book analyzes the case law generated by student dress-code litigation with the goal of identifying the themes that have emerged in the various court decisions. It is our hope that this book will contribute to a better understanding of the legal issues surrounding school districts' dress codes as well as provide practical guidance to school authorities for drafting and implementing a student dress code that will withstand a legal challenge.

NOTES

1. Todd A. DeMitchell, Richard Fossey, & Casey Cobb, "Dress Codes in the Public Schools: Principals, Policies, and Precepts." 29 *Journal of Law & Education* 31, 45 (2000).

2. Defoe Ex Rel. Defoe v. Spiva, 625 F.3d 324, 326 (6th Cir. 2010).

3. Ibid.

4. Ibid., 327.

5. Ibid., 329 (Rogers, J. concurring).

6. Ibid., 330 (Rogers, J. concurring).

7. Ibid., 339 (Rogers, J. concurring).

8. Ibid (Rogers, J. concurring) (emphasis in original).

9. Ibid. (Rogers, J.).

10. Ibid (Roger, J. concurring).

11. Gilman v. School Board for Holmes County, 567 F. Supp. 2d 1359, 1365 (N.D. Fla. 2008).

12. Dreaming Bear v. Fleming, 714 F. Supp. 2d 972, 975 (D.S.D. 2010).

13. E-mail communication discussing the "4 Bs" dress code in the possession of co-author DeMitchell from Ashley Mancusi (January 16, 2013).

14. Harper v. Edgewood Board of Education, 655 F. Supp. 1353 (S.D. Ohio 1987).

15. Olesen v. Board of Education of School District No. 228, 676 F. Supp. 820 (N.D. Ill. 1987). In Hines v. Caston School Corp., 651 N.E.2d (Ind. Ct. App. 1995), suit was brought by a male elementary school student challenging a school policy banning the wearing of earrings by boys. The suit was brought under due process and equal protection grounds, not free speech. The court held that the law was reasonably related to the desire of the community's schools to reflect its values and instill discipline. Wearing earrings by males was considered inconsistent with community standards.

16. McMillen v. Itawamba County School District, 702 F. Supp. 2d 699, 705 (N.D. Miss. 2010). For a discussion of proms and LGBT students, *see* Suzanne Eckes, Todd DeMitchell, & Richard Fossey, Commentary: "A White Sports Coat and a Pink Carnation: Protecting the Legal Rights of LGBT Students to Attend the Prom," *Teachers College Record* (March 29, 2013), available at http://www.tcrecord.org ID Number 17072. *Also see* Doe ex rel. Doe v. Yunits, No. 001060A, 2000 WL 33162199 (Mass. Super. Oct. 11, 2000), in which a Massachusetts public school district was enjoined from prohibiting a male student from attending school wearing female clothes and accoutrements.

17. Rob Killen, "The Achilles' Heel of Dress Codes: The Definition of Proper Attire in Public Schools," 36 *Tulsa Law Journal* 459 (2000).

18. Bivens v. Albuquerque Public Schools, 899 F. Supp. 556, 559 (D.N.M. 1995).

TWO

Free Speech Rights of Students

When I asked [Justice William J. Brennan] if he had a favorite part of
the Constitution, he replied, "The First Amendment, I expect. All other
liberties and rights flow from the freedom to speak up. Its enforcement
gives us this society. The other provisions of the Constitution merely
embellish it."

—Nate Hentoff[1]

FROM REASONABLENESS TO CONSTITUTIONAL CONSTRAINTS: AN EVOLVING UNDERSTANDING OF SCHOOLS' AUTHORITY OVER THEIR STUDENTS

Schools and the courts have come a long way from the time when a state
court upheld a school rule that prohibited Pearl Pugsley, an Arkansas
high school student, from wearing talcum powder on her face while she
was at school. In a 1923 decision, the Arkansas Supreme Court ruled that
a school rule banning students from wearing transparent hosiery, face
paint, cosmetics, or immodest dress[2] was reasonable and did not involve
"oppression or humiliation."

At the same time, the Arkansas Supreme Court voiced concern about
being drawn into a school dispute involving a student's cosmetics.
"Courts have other and more important functions to perform than that of
hearing the complaints of dissatisfied pupils of the public schools against
rules and regulations promulgated by the school boards for the government of the schools,"[3] the court wrote.

However, one Arkansas judge dissented in the case, asserting that
Pearl was eighteen years old and any school rule forbidding a student of
her age from wearing talcum powder as a cosmetic was unreasonable

and an abuse of authority. "Useless laws diminish the authority of the necessary ones," he wrote.[4]

Under the law as asserted by the Arkansas Supreme Court in the *Pugsley* case, school officials needed only act reasonably when enacting and enforcing student dress codes. They were not required to secure the constitutional rights of their students. Through the first half of the twentieth century, reasonableness was the near universal standard for the regulation of student conduct in the schools. The courts were "very reluctant to declare a board's student-conduct regulation to be unreasonable," even when the court believed that the regulation was "unwise" or "inexpedient."[5] *reasonableness was the standard*

This reasonableness standard was articulated again and again by U.S. courts during the first half of the twentieth century. In a 1908 case, for example, the Wisconsin Supreme Court upheld the suspension of a student who ridiculed his teacher in a poem published in the local newspaper. The court stated that school authorities must be invested with broad authority to discipline students unless that authority "has been illegally or unreasonably exercised."[6]

the change But times have changed. Schools still have a duty to refrain from acting in an arbitrary, capricious, or discriminatory manner toward their students. But in addition, they also have a duty to respect their students' constitutional rights.

Over the years, the United States Supreme Court has clearly affirmed that students have constitutional rights when they are on school premises that school authorities must respect. For example, students have a constitutional right to privacy under the Fourth Amendment, which they do not give up when they come on school grounds; and school officials cannot disregard that right simply because they desire to search a student's person or possessions.[7] Students also have a constitutional right to due process before being suspended or expelled from school.[8] Of course they also enjoy the constitutional right to equal protection under the law and cannot be discriminated against based on their race or color.[9]

And students also have a constitutional right to free speech under the First Amendment, a right they do not relinquish when they walk through the schoolhouse gate. Commencing with *Tinker v. Des Moines Community Independent School District* in 1969,[10] the United States Supreme Court has issued four opinions articulating the constitutional rights of students in the schools. Applying principles set down by the Supreme Court, the lower courts have decided dozens of cases involving the free speech rights of students.

Of course, students' constitutional rights are subject to some limitations in the school environment—particularly their right to freedom of speech. After all, schools have a legal responsibility to provide an environment conducive to learning. Therefore, a student's First Amendment right to free speech must be "balanced against the need to foster an educational atmosphere free from undue disruptions to appropriate discipline."[11]

DO STUDENTS HAVE A CONSTITUTIONAL RIGHT TO CHOOSE WHAT THEY WEAR TO SCHOOL?

The Supreme Court's *Tinker* decision firmly established that students have a constitutional right to expression when they are at school so long as the speech is not disruptive and does not interfere with the rights of others. When the Supreme Court decided the *Tinker* case in 1969, the justices may not have anticipated that the *Tinker* decision would be cited not only in support of a student's constitutional right to speak, but also to advance the claim that students have a constitutional right to choose what they wear to school.

Since time immemorial, schools have required students to abide by dress codes that require students to dress modestly and to adhere to school standards for cleanliness and neatness. For example, boys might be required to tuck their shirttails inside their pants and girls might be prohibited from wearing immodestly short skirts. Until the 1970s, no one saw any constitutional implications to student dress codes.

In the wake of the *Tinker* decision, however, students began bringing lawsuits against school districts claiming that their clothing choices amounted to constitutionally protected expression. In some of these cases, students claimed a right to proclaim explicit messages on their clothing; but in other cases, they argued for the right to choose clothing that proclaimed their identity or simply made them feel good about themselves.

At the same time student-clothing litigation was emerging, school districts began adopting more and more explicit student dress codes; and some went further and required students to wear prescribed uniforms to school. Schools began regulating student dress more stringently in order to address problems of discipline and security, to make school expectations about student dress more explicit, and perhaps to cut down on litigation. Unfortunately, in many instances, this strategy often resulted in more litigation in which educators and students were required to spend time in court rather than in the classroom.

In a time of concern for civility in society, respect for legitimate authority, and security for schoolchildren, the debate about dress codes has often been sharp. This debate highlights important questions about the constitutional right of students to express themselves through their clothing or through messages on their clothing—typically T-shirts.

Do we as a society value the rights of students to wear clothes of their choice to school even when many adults would consider the clothing vulgar and offensive? Do students have the right to proclaim social and political messages on their clothing? In short, do students possess a constitutional right of freedom of expression to wear clothes of their choice to school; and if so, to what extent do educators possess the authority to limit that right?

An understanding of a student's First Amendment rights in the school environment is a necessary predicate for a discussion about the constitutionality of school regulations on students' dress. Thus far, the United States Supreme Court has not decided a case involving the constitutionality of a school's student dress code. However, in four opinions stretching over a period of almost forty years, the High Court has outlined the parameters of a student's constitutional right of expression in the public schools, and lower courts have looked to these four opinions for guidance when deciding lawsuits on the constitutionality of school dress codes. Lower courts have also drawn on certain Supreme Court decisions on the constitutional right of expression that were decided outside the context of education.

It is appropriate to look at the important Supreme Court decisions that bear on a student's right to free expression before we examine the school-clothing litigation in detail. Thus, this chapter is devoted to a review of students' broad right to freedom of expression in the schools. Later chapters will examine court decisions dealing specifically with constitutional challenges to school districts' restrictions on what students wear to school.

STUDENTS AND THE CONSTITUTION: THE RIGHT TO FREE SPEECH

Students have not always possessed the right to free speech in the school environment. In fact "the United States Supreme Court did not even apply the Bill of Rights to public school students until the 1940s."[12] In *Tinker v. Des Moines Community Independent School District*, however, the Supreme Court made clear that students do in fact possess a First Amendment right to freedom of speech that they do not relinquish when they enter the schoolhouse.

In succeeding opinions, the Supreme Court sketched out the scope and limitations of a student's free speech rights while at school. Including the *Tinker* decision, there are now four United States Supreme Court decisions that structure the free speech rights of public school students.

Moreover, there has been a creep of non-education cases into student free speech jurisprudence. In several cases, federal courts have drawn on free speech cases outside the school context to reach decisions about the limitations on a student's First Amendment rights in the school environment. In particular, lower courts have cited non-education Supreme Court cases in cases involving school-uniform and school dress-code cases. Consequently, we will explore several non-education Supreme Court decisions that have been cited in student speech cases. But we will begin our discussion with an overview of the First Amendment.

Free Speech: The First Amendment

Freedom of speech is arguably the touchstone of our conception of individual liberty. It is a cherished value vigorously protected in our society. Justice Cardozo characterized it as "the matrix, the indispensable condition of nearly every other form of freedom."[13] The right to free speech is extensive and robust.[14] As Justice Holmes observed, "it is . . . not free thought for those who agree with us, but freedom for the thought that we hate."[15]

Moreover, free speech does not lose its constitutional protection simply because it might provoke unpleasantness or unrest. As the Supreme Court noted, "[a] function of free speech under our system of government is to invite dispute. It may indeed best serve its high purpose when it induces a condition of unrest, creates dissatisfaction with conditions as they are, or even stirs people to anger. Speech is often provocative and challenging."[16]

However, there are restrictions on the constitutional right to free speech; it is not absolute. The courts, when reviewing free speech challenges, must parse the difference between the reasonable regulation of speech and the suppression of speech. As a general rule, the government may not suppress the expression of ideas, except in very specific circumstances when expression constitutes so-called fighting words,[17] incitement to riot producing imminent lawless action,[18] defamation,[19] and child pornography.[20]

However, "[i]f there is a bedrock principle underlying the First Amendment, it is that government may not prohibit the expression of an idea simply because society finds the idea itself offensive or disagreeable."[21] A government regulation containing content-related restrictions faces a presumption against its validity. An assessment of whether a regulation is content related or content neutral depends on "whether the government has adopted a regulation of speech because of disagreement with the message it conveys."[22]

An example of government suppressing speech through a content-related regulation is found in *R.A.V. v. St. Paul*, in which the St. Paul Bias-Motivated Crime Ordinance was struck down.[23] The ordinance was used to prosecute someone for burning a cross on the lawn of an African American family. While the Supreme Court, in a somewhat fractured opinion, found the act to be reprehensible, it also found that that the ordinance suppressed speech.

Governmental agencies that promulgate content-related regulations that suppress speech come to the courts with a heavy burden of proving

[handwritten margin note: Dress that codes are content neutral greater chance success]

[handwritten margin note: neutral]

constitutionality, while content-neutral regulations generally shoulder a lighter load. If a dress code is considered content neutral—in other words, it is not aimed at suppressing specific speech—it has a greater chance of success. An example is the dress code passed by the Waxahachie Independent School District in which all shirts containing printed messages were banned (except for messages pertaining to school spirit and approved by the principal).[24] All shirt-based speech was prohibited; thus, the regulation did not single out a particular message to suppress. The Fifth Circuit Court of Appeals upheld the constitutionality of the school district's dress code since it was content neutral and had not been promulgated to suppress student expression.

In *Tinker v. Des Moines Independent Community School District*, decided more than forty years ago, the Supreme Court held that students do not shed their constitutional right to free speech at the schoolhouse gate.[25] The court struck a balance between the "scrupulous protection of Constitutional freedoms of the individual"[26] and the compelling need for the public schools to perform their proper educational function. The United States Supreme Court argued for a robust right of free speech for public school students, eschewing a mere shadow of a right. As the Supreme Court wrote,

> Any departure from absolute regimentation may cause trouble. Any variation from the majority's opinion may inspire fear. Any word spoken, in class, in the lunchroom, or on the campus, that deviates from the views of another person may start an argument or cause a disturbance. But our Constitution says we must take the risk, and our history says that it is this sort of hazardous freedom—this kind of openness—that is the basis of our national strength and of the independence and vigor of American who grow up and live in this relatively permissive, often disputatious society.[27]

The Public School as a Special Place

Even though students do not shed their constitutional right to free speech at the schoolhouse gate, they do not receive the same measure of protections for their free speech as adults. "Students are free to express themselves in many ways outside the schoolhouse gate, but inside the schoolhouse gate it is another matter."[28] Restrictions are placed on children that are greater than those placed on adults.[29] Similarly, a student's Fourth Amendment search and seizure rights inside the schoolhouse gate are not identical to those of adults.[30]

In *Tinker*, the Supreme Court emphasized that a student's right to free speech in the school environment must be exercised "within the special circumstances of the school environment."[31] Thus the *Tinker* decision and the numerous court decisions that have interpreted *Tinker* over the years give appropriate deference to school administrators' judgment as to what speech is appropriate in the context of the public school.[32]

Indeed, the courts have been loath to intervene in the decisions of school boards unless it can be shown that the board acted in an arbitrary, capricious, or unreasonable manner. School boards have a substantial interest in creating and maintaining a safe and effective learning environment, and the federal courts have often acknowledged this fact.

Moreover, schools have the authority to inculcate fundamental civic values into their curricular programs and have absolute discretion to develop a curriculum that reflects those values.[33] These fundamental values include "habits and manners of civility." Although toleration of divergent views and unpopular views is important to civility, sensibilities of others, including teachers and fellow students, are also important.[34] As Justice Burger explained, a student's freedom to advocate unpopular and controversial views in schools and classrooms "must be balanced against the society's countervailing interest in teaching students the boundaries of socially appropriate behavior."[35] Therefore, "[e]ven the most heated political discourse in a democratic society requires consideration for the personal sensibilities of the other participants and audiences.[36]

In short, a student's right to free speech in the school environment is not absolute. As outlined in later chapters of this book, the federal courts have been called upon repeatedly in the years since the *Tinker* case was decided to determine the exact contours of a student's free speech rights while at school, in the context of specific conflicts with school authorities who assert their need to control student speech in order to maintain a safe and orderly learning environment.

THE SUPREME COURT'S FOUR STUDENT FREE-SPEECH CASES

The Black Armband Case: Tinker v. Des Moines

The Supreme Court first recognized a student's right to free speech in the school environment more than forty years ago in the landmark decision of *Tinker v. Des Moines Independent Community School District*.[37] The case involved facts that occurred in 1965, when Des Moines School officials suspended John and Mary Beth Tinker and Chris Eckhart for wearing black armbands to school in protest of the Vietnam War. The school administration had learned about the Tinker children's planned protest in advance and hastily developed and implemented a policy targeting the protest. The three students brought suit in federal court arguing that the First Amendment gave them the right to express themselves in this quiet and dignified way.

The federal district court dismissed their complaint. On appeal, the Eighth Circuit Court of Appeals heard the case *en banc* but the court was equally divided. The Tinkers then proceeded to the United State Supreme Court to press their case that they had a constitutional right to quietly and passively wear a two-inch-wide black armband in protest of the war in Vietnam.

In its 1969 decision, the Supreme Court declared that "[s]tudents in school as well as out of school are 'persons' under the Constitution. They are possessed of fundamental rights that the state must respect, just as they themselves must respect their obligations to the State."[38] Although, school officials possess "the comprehensive authority . . . to prescribe and control conduct in the schools,"[39] they must exercise that authority within the bounds of the Constitution.

"In our system," the Court emphasized, "state-operated schools may not be enclaves of totalitarianism."[40] Thus "students may not be regarded as closed-circuit recipients of only that which the State chooses to communicate. They may not be confined to the expression of those sentiments that are officially approved."[41]

The Supreme Court found that school authorities could not justify the prohibition of student expression unless the conduct would "materially and substantially interfere with the requirements of appropriate discipline in the operation of the school" or "collid[e] with the rights of others."[42] The Court asserted that "undifferentiated fear or apprehension of disturbance" cannot trump this "hazardous freedom" and replace it with rigid regimentation.[43]

Using this line of reasoning, school authorities cannot restrict a student's clothing that arguably has some symbolic or explicit expression unless they can show that the clothing might "materially disrupts classwork," provoke "substantial disorder" in the school environment,[44] or interfere with " the rights of other students to be secure and to be let alone."[45]

Courts have cited *Tinker* many times over the years in cases involving the free expression rights of public school students in their choice of clothing and appearance. Unfortunately, few of these cases involved issues as noble as the one the Tinkers brought forward. In fact, as discussed in succeeding chapters, the Supreme Court's *Tinker* decision has been cited more than once by plaintiff students for the proposition that students have an unfettered right to wear what they choose to school regardless of whether the clothing conveys an important social or political message.

In *Tinker*, the Supreme Court expressly differentiated between a school's restrictions on a student's constitutionally protected speech and a school's dress code. In fact, the Court emphasized that "[t]he problem posed by the present case does not relate to regulation of the length of skirts or the type of clothing. Our problem involves direct, primary First Amendment rights akin to 'pure speech.'"[46]

Nevertheless, in spite of the fact that the Supreme Court implicitly differentiated between pure speech and clothing issues, several courts have cited *Tinker* for the proposition that a student's choice of clothing style carries the protection of the United States Constitution. For example, only a year after the *Tinker* decision, a New Hampshire sixth grader persuaded a federal court that he had a liberty interest in wearing blue jeans to school, even though he had violated the school's dress code.[47] Although the judge admitted that the constitutional interest was minor, he ruled that the school district had not justified its infringement on a child's right to choose his own pants.[48]

Bethel School District v. Fraser: *"I know a man who is firm."*[49]

In *Tinker*, the Supreme Court held that students have free speech rights on the school grounds that cannot be restricted so long as the speech is not disruptive and does not interfere with the rights of other students. In the years since *Tinker*, however, the court has issued three opinions that have approved certain restrictions on students' free speech rights while at school, allowing school officials to censor some categories of free speech, even when the speech is not disruptive.

Seventeen years after *Tinker*, the Supreme Court decided a case that would dramatically impact students' rights of expression at school. In *Bethel School District No. 403 v. Fraser,* the Supreme Court ruled that school officials could sanction a high school student for using lewd, vulgar, or offensive sexual metaphors during a political speech at a school assembly.[50] In that case, Mathew Fraser gave a nomination speech at a student assembly that was filled with graphic language laden with explicit sexual references. Some students in the school assembly "hooted and yelled" and made sexual gestures in response to his speech, while other students sat bewildered and embarrassed.

After a due process hearing with the assistant principal, Fraser received a three-day suspension for using obscene language in violation of the school's discipline code, and he had his name removed from the graduation candidates' speaker list.[51] Fraser contested the discipline in federal district court, alleging a violation of the First Amendment right to free speech.

The district court held for Fraser, asserting that the school's disruptive conduct rule was vague and overbroad. It awarded Fraser $278 in damages and $12,750 in litigation costs and attorney's fees. The school district appealed but lost at the Ninth Circuit Court of Appeals. The circuit court found that Fraser's speech was "indistinguishable" from Tinker's armband.[52]

The school district then appealed the Ninth Circuit's decision to the U.S. Supreme Court, which reversed the Ninth Circuit and ruled that school officials had the authority to sanction Fraser for his offensive speech. In ruling for the school district, the Supreme Court chose not apply the *Tinker* standard of material and substantial disruption, and instead fashioned a new analysis and test. The Supreme Court stated emphatically that the public schools have the duty to "inculcate[s] the habits and manners of civility."[53] This fundamental value of civility, the Court pointed out, must take into account the "sensibilities of others."[54] Thus, schools need not tolerate in the school environment student speech that is lewd or vulgar.

Even the nation's senior political leaders, the Supreme Court pointed out, have rules against offensive expression in America's legislative halls, where vigorous political debate often occurs. "Can it be," the Court asked, "that what is proscribed in the halls of Congress is beyond the reach of school officials to regulate?"[55]

In *Fraser*, the Supreme Court ruled that "[t]he determination of what manner of speech in the classroom or in a school assembly is inappropriate properly rests with the school board."[56] Thus, the Court upheld a school district's right to prohibit speech that is lewd, offensive, or vulgar. "Surely it is a highly appropriate function of public education to prohibit vulgar and offensive terms in public discourse."[57]

Furthermore, the Court affirmed that the constitutional rights of students in public schools are not automatically coextensive with the rights of adults in other settings. While adults have wide freedom in matters of public discourse, it does not follow that the same latitude must be permitted to children in Pre-K–12 public schools.

Although the Supreme Court's decision has been cited less frequently than *Tinker* by the lower courts when deciding student clothing cases, *Fraser* is applied to student clothing that the courts deem vulgar. For example, the Sixth Circuit Court of Appeals applied the Supreme Court's rationale in *Fraser* in ruling that a student's Marilyn Manson T-shirt, which portrayed a three-headed Jesus and proclaimed the words "See No Truth, Hear No Truth, Speak No Truth" was vulgar, offensive, and contrary to the mission of the school.[58] Because the T-shirt was vulgar, the Sixth Circuit reasoned, it was not necessary to determine whether wearing the T-shirt to school might disrupt the school environment.

Hazelwood *and a Legitimate Pedagogical Concern*

Fraser reduced some of the reach of *Tinker* by adding speech that is lewd, vulgar, and offensive to the types of speech that school authorities can ban without violating the First Amendment. Thus, in addition to student speech that school authorities reasonably believe is disruptive, school officials can ban speech that is patently offensive.

A third important Supreme Court case, *Hazelwood School District v. Kuhlmeier*,[59] added further restrictions on students' right to free speech in the school setting. *Hazelwood* involved the question of whether students have a constitutional right to make unilateral decisions about what appears in a student newspaper that was produced as part of a high school journalism class.

In this case, student contributors to a school newspaper published as part of a journalism class contested the principal's decision to delete articles from the newspaper prior to its publication, based on the principal's judgment that the articles were either inappropriate for the school's younger students to read or were not produced in accordance with established principles of professional journalism.

In their lawsuit against the school district, the students claimed the newspaper was an open forum, somewhat similar to traditional open forums such as streets and parks, which are commonly open to assembly and communication, with minimal governmental restrictions. Since the newspaper was a public forum, the students contended, they enjoyed the constitutional right to determine what the newspaper should print, without censorship by school authorities.

In deciding the case, the Supreme Court concluded that a high school's student newspaper is not an open forum as the students had argued. Rather, the newspaper, which was produced in a journalism class, formed part of the curriculum and was school-sponsored speech. Regarding such speech, the Court ruled, "school officials may impose reasonable restrictions on the speech of students, teachers, and other members of the school community."[60]

Since the school was not an open forum for student expression, the school newspaper, as part of its curriculum (the speech of the school), was not a forum for indiscriminate student speech. The school, as a forum for speech, is "reserved for its intended purpose of creating supervised learning experiences."[61] The *Hazelwood* court found that the school had authority over such school-sponsored publications as theatrical productions and "other expressive activities that students, parents, and other members of the public might reasonably perceive to bear the imprimatur of the school."[62] The Supreme Court held that educators do not offend the Constitution by exercising editorial control over school-sponsored expression "so long as their actions are reasonably related to legitimate pedagogical concerns."[63]

Deference to school authorities was given full weight when the Court reasoned, "We thus recognize that the determination of what manner of speech in the classroom or in school assembly is appropriate properly rests with the school board rather than the federal courts."[64] Consequently, "[a] school need not tolerate student speech that is inconsistent with its 'basic educational mission.'"[65]

Morse v. Frederick: *Bong Hits 4 Jesus*

The latest Supreme Court student speech case is *Morse v. Frederick,* sometimes known as the "Bong Hits 4 Jesus" case.[66] On January 24, 2002, the Olympic Torch Relay passed through Juneau, Alaska, on the way to the Salt Lake City Winter Olympics. The route went past Juneau-Douglas High School, and the principal allowed students and staff to view the event outdoors as part of a school-sponsored event. School supervision was provided.

Joseph Frederick, a student at the school, was late for class and joined some of his classmates across the street from the school. When the torch-bearers and camera crew passed by, Frederick and several of his friends unfurled a banner proclaiming "Bong Hits 4 Jesus," apparently hoping they would be filmed by the television crew.

The banner could easily be seen from the school grounds. When Deborah Morse, the high school principal, spotted the banner, she immediately crossed the street and ordered the students to stop displaying it. All of the students, with the exception of Frederick, complied. Frederick was ordered to the principal's office and was subsequently suspended. Principal Morse asserted that the banner advocated the use of illegal drugs, which was in violation of the school's policy. Frederick sued Morse and the school district in federal court, claiming a violation of his First Amendment rights.

A federal district court in Juneau, Alaska, granted summary judgment to the school defendants.[67] Frederick then appealed to the Ninth Circuit Court of Appeals, which reversed.[68] The Ninth Circuit ruled that Morse had violated young Frederick's clearly established First Amendment rights and that he could sue Morse personally for money damages.

The case then proceeded to the United Supreme Court, which reversed the Ninth Circuit's opinion.[69] The High Court discussed the rulings in *Tinker, Bethel,* and *Hazelwood* but found them inapplicable to the case before it. The court instead looked to another line of Supreme Court cases to anchor its decision. The message of Frederick's banner could reasonably be construed as condoning or advocating drug use, the Court said. (Frederick himself contended that the words were "nonsense meant to attract the television cameras."[70])

Consequently, the Court turned to two prior Fourth Amendment student drug testing cases, *Vernonia School District 47J v. Acton*[71] and *Board of Education v. Earls,*[72] for guidance. In *Vernonia,* the court had approved a school district's random drug testing policy for student athletes; and in *Earls,* the court upheld a school district's random drug testing program for students participating in extracurricular activities.

Vernonia and *Earls* both recognized that schools have an important governmental interest in stopping students from using drugs, the Supreme Court observed. Moreover, "Congress has declared that part of a school's job is educating students about the dangers of illegal drug use." The Court pointed out that Congress had "provided billions of dollars to support state and local drug-prevention programs . . . and required that schools receiving federal funds under the Safe and Drug-Free Schools and Communities Act of 1995 certify that their drug prevention programs 'convey a clear and consistent message . . . that illegal use of drugs is wrong and harmful.'"[73] Indeed, the Juneau school board and thousands of school boards all over the United States had adopted policies to deter the illegal use of drugs among students.

Thus, in the Supreme Court's majority view as expressed by Justice Roberts, the special characteristics of the school environment and the strong governmental interest in stopping students from using drugs allow schools to "restrict student expression that they reasonably regard as promoting illegal drug use."[74] In fact, the Court asserted, "failing to act would send a powerful message to the students in [the principal's] charge . . . about how serious the school was about the dangers of illegal drug use."[75]

In concluding his opinion, Justice Roberts acknowledged the challenges that school administrators face. "School principals have a difficult job, and a vitally important one." Justice Roberts continued:

> When Frederick suddenly and unexpectedly unfurled his banner, Morse had to decide to act — or not act — on the spot. It was reasonable for her to conclude that the banner promoted illegal drug use — in violation of established school policy — and that failing to act would send a powerful message to the students in her charge, including Frederick, about how seriously the school was about the dangers of illegal drug use. The First Amendment does not require schools to tolerate at school events student expression that contributes to those dangers.[76]

In short, the Supreme Court's majority opinion in *Morse v. Frederick* strongly affirmed the authority of school officials to ban student expression in the school environment or at school-sponsored activities that officials reasonably interpret as promoting illegal drug use. Although the *Morse* case dealt with a banner, not a T-shirt, this authority clearly includes the right to prohibit students from displaying messages on their clothing that celebrate or promote the use of illegal drugs. Moreover, although the Supreme Court's opinion did not mention the illegal use of alcohol, the opinion's reasoning at least implies that school authorities can prohibit student expression that celebrates or promotes the underage use of alcoholic beverages.

Thus, school administrators should make sure their school policies explicitly state that student expression that promotes or celebrates the use of illegal drugs or alcohol is prohibited in the school environment and all school-sponsored functions. Then, if "Bong Hits 4 Jesus" or a similar drug-celebrating phrase appears on a banner or a student's T-shirt, school officials can constitutionally rely on that policy to take appropriate action to remove the offending message from the school environment without violating the First Amendment.

It will likely take a number of years for lower court decisions to determine the full implications of the *Morse* decision and to establish its place among the Supreme Court's three previous cases on the free speech rights of students in the schools.[77] However, one commentator opined that *Morse* does not "mark a major doctrinal shift in student free speech."[78]

In summary, the Supreme Court has fashioned four tests that are used in student free speech cases. Typically, courts review speech that is lewd, vulgar, or offensive using the *Fraser* standard. School-sponsored speech is analyzed under *Hazelwood,* and student speech that promotes drugs or illegal activities is reviewed under *Morse's* standard. All other speech is reviewed under the *Tinker* standard to determine whether the student speech caused a substantial disruption or was likely to cause such a disruption. Together, these four Supreme Court decisions make clear that a student's right to free speech in the school environment is not absolute, nor is it coextensive with the free speech rights of adults. Students have the right to freedom of speech in school, but that right must be balanced with the legitimate interest of school authorities to efficiently and effectively provide instruction to their students.

NON-EDUCATION FREE SPEECH CASES

The four student free speech tests fashioned by the Supreme Court reflect the finding that the public school is a special place. Consequently, because it is special, the constitutional tests that are fashioned by the courts must address the school context when ruling on disputes between school authorities and students over student expression in the schools.

While the four big cases dominate student free speech analysis, there is an emerging use of non-education jurisprudence to work through the balancing act of student free speech and school efficiency and effectiveness. We will explore the non-education cases, which have primarily been used in school-uniform cases but are also surfacing in dress-code cases.

These cases are important in school-uniform and dress-code cases because they focus on what constitutes speech in cases where students argue that nonverbal expression and nonverbal activities are entitled to First Amendment protection. If some activity is not considered speech, the protection of the First Amendment free speech clause cannot be asserted. The centrality of this initial analysis is found in *Tinker*. In *Tinker,* the Supreme Court first had to find that students have a constitutional right to free speech, and then it had to decide whether the black armband was speech. The Court decided in the affirmative on both issues. Wearing the black armband in protest of the war in Vietnam is a symbolic act "akin to pure speech."[79] We will explore the most pertinent non-education cases below.

United States v. O'Brien: *Burning a Draft Card*[80]

David Paul O'Brien, accompanied by three companions, burned his draft card on the steps of the South Boston courthouse in a symbolic gesture against the draft. O'Brien was attacked by members of the crowd. Several agents of the Federal Bureau of Investigation who were part of the crowd ushered O'Brien and his companions into the safety of the courthouse where he was arrested, and later indicted, tried, convicted, and sentenced in federal court. His act violated the 1948 (amended in 1965) Universal Military Training and Service Act, which made it an offense to alter, destroy, or mutilate a draft card. He brought suit alleging that the statute suppressed his free speech rights.

The Supreme Court faced the issue of whether O'Brien's conduct was speech. Chief Justice Warren, writing for the Court stated, "We cannot accept the view that an apparently limitless variety of conduct can be labeled 'speech' whenever the person engaging in the conduct intends thereby to express an idea."[81] Even the intent to communicate does not transform every act into expression that is protected by the First Amendment.

Even arguing that burning the draft card was speech, O'Brien had to prevail on the postulation that the statute's purpose was to suppress speech.[82] The Supreme Court asked whether the statute furthered an important or substantial governmental interest that is unrelated to the suppression of free expression and whether any "incidental" restriction was no greater than is necessary to meet the governmental interest.[83] The Court found that the statute met a substantial governmental interest that was not related to the suppression of speech. Therefore, when he burned his draft card, O'Brien frustrated the governmental interest in enforcing the selective service laws.

The *O'Brien* test essentially determines whether the disputed governmental regulation is justified by asking three questions. First, does the regulation further a governmental interest? Second, is the government's interest unrelated to the suppression of free speech? Third, is the government's interest greater than any incidental suppression of speech?

A number of circuits courts have used *O'Brien* in their analysis.[84] Whereas *Tinker* reviews a particular student expression to determine whether it creates a substantial disruption, *O'Brien* reviews the challenged school regulation to determine whether it passes constitutional muster under the three-part test set forth above.

An example of the application of the *O'Brien* test in the school context is found in a federal district court decision involving a Kentucky high school.[85] The Atherton High School Site Based Decision Making Council adopted a school policy to support an environment that maximized student achievement. The council addressed a rising concern about student dress that might signal gang identification or promote violence. As a result, a dress code was enacted that limited clothing choices and prohibited clothing logos except for the school's logo. Medallions and necklaces were also banned. Students who alleged that the dress code prevented expressive conduct by limiting clothing choices brought a free speech lawsuit.

The federal district court applied the *O'Brien* test to the school district's content-neutral dress code policy.[86] The court first concluded that school officials have an "important and substantial interest in creating an appropriate learning environment by preventing gang presence and limiting fights in school."[87] Second, school authorities had not adopted the dress code for the purpose of suppressing student speech. Third, any student speech that was suppressed by the dress code was incidental and outweighed by the school's goal of creating a safe and peaceful learning environment. In this part of its analysis, the court took note of the fact that the dress code policy "does not prohibit alternative and more specific student expression through badges, buttons and other means."[88] In other words, student speech was not totally stifled by the policy; there were alternate avenues for student expression. The dress code was reasonably related to a legitimate objective, the court concluded.

Spence v. Washington: *The Peace Symbol and the American Flag*[89]

On appeal from the Supreme Court of Washington, the United States Supreme Court heard the case of a college student who responded to the 1970 invasion of Cambodia and student killings at Kent State University by affixing, through removable tape, a large peace symbol (three feet by five feet) to the American flag. The student hung the flag upside down with the peace symbol outside his apartment window. His purpose was to associate the flag with peace instead of war and violence. His action violated a Washington statute forbidding the exhibition of the American flag with attached or superimposed figures or symbols. He was convicted of violating the statute.[90]

The Supreme Court, citing *Tinker*, noted that the symbol of the flag and peace sign were symbols of expression. "[I]t was a pointed expression of anguish by appellant about the then-current domestic and foreign affairs of his government. An intent to convey a particularized message was present, and in the surrounding circumstances the likelihood was great that the message would be understood by those who viewed it."[91] Consequently, the Court cast the case as one of prosecution of an idea through an activity. It is interesting to note that the Court found *O'Brien* to be "inapplicable" because no other governmental interest unrelated to expression was advanced or supported by the Washington statute.[92]

Spence meant to communicate his ideas using the American flag. Thus, he sought to communicate his protest through the symbolism of an altered American flag. According to the Supreme Court, his act "was not an act of mindless nihilism."[93] It was the sort of communication through symbols that was a "short-cut from mind to mind."[94]

The *Spence* test states that for a symbolic act to qualify as expression, and thus protection under the First Amendment, it must be "imbued with elements of communication" that convey a "particularized message" that would most likely be understood. Essentially, *Spence* established a test for the constitutional protection of the use of symbols as speech. It is important to note that the *Spence* court found a lowered governmental interest in controlling expression because the speech took place on private property rather than on property over which government exercised supervisory control.[95] This may have implications for schools, since school authorities exercise control over student expression inside the schoolhouse gate that they could not exercise outside the gate.

Spence has been applied in school settings. For example, in *Isaacs v. Board of Education*, a student asserted that her headwrap celebrated her African American and Jamaican heritage and thus should be exempt from the school's no hats/headgear policy.[96] In the court's view, however, the student failed the *Spence* test; the court was not convinced that the wearing of a headwrap conveyed a particularized message about the student's heritage that other students would understand.

Texas v. Johnson: *Burning the American Flag*[97]

Gregory Lee Johnson unfurled the American flag in front of the Dallas City Hall during the time that the 1984 Republican National Convention was taking place in Dallas. He doused the flag with kerosene and set it on fire.[98] He was part of a group of around one hundred demonstrators who were protesting policies of the Reagan administration. There was neither disruption nor a breach of the peace following the flag burning. Johnson was arrested, charged, and convicted of violating the Texas penal code, which made it a crime to desecrate a venerated object. An intermediate Texas appellate court affirmed the conviction, but the Texas Court of Criminal Appeals reversed, recognizing Johnson's speech as symbolic given the circumstances.

The United States Supreme Court granted certiorari and heard the case. The Court began by asking the question raised in *Spence*: Did Johnson's expressive conduct constitute speech? Next the Court followed *O'Brien* and asked whether the State's regulation was related to the suppression of free expression.

In analyzing the case, the Supreme Court concluded that Johnson's burning of the American flag was related to a political demonstration that coincided with the Republican Party's renomination of President Reagan and was not a random act. "The expressive, overtly political nature of [Johnson's] conduct was both intentional and overwhelmingly apparent."[99] Second, the Court held that government "has a freer hand in restricting expressive conduct than it does in restricting the written or spoken word."[100] Nevertheless, in the instant case, the Court asserted that government cannot appropriate specific symbols to be used only for the purposes designated by government "to communicate a limited set of messages would be to enter territory having no discernible or defensible boundaries."[101]

It was not the state's asserted goal—preservation of the flag as the symbol of our country—with which the justices took issue. Rather, it was the government's means of trying to achieve that goal, which was to criminalize the behavior of a citizen who used the revered symbol of the American flag to convey a message that was different from the one the state preferred. The Court did not believe that the special role that the American flag plays in American life was endangered by the act of a solitary person.

The Court acknowledged that the American Flag is a symbol with great transcendent meaning for the majority of Americans. Nevertheless, the Court observed, "The way to preserve the flag's special role is not to punish those who feel differently about these matters. It is to persuade them that they are wrong."[102] The individual's right to free speech encompasses the communication of "offensive and disagreeable" ideas.[103]

The Supreme Court asked two questions as part of its analysis. First, did Johnson intend to convey a particularized message when he burned an American flag? The Court then asked whether there was likelihood that the people who viewed the message would understand Johnson's message.[104] The answer to both questions, the Court concluded, was yes.

An example of the use of *Texas v. Johnson* in an education context is *Governor Wentworth Regional School District v. Hendrickson.*[105] This case, discussed in greater detail in chapter 4, involved an ongoing dispute between two groups of students in a New Hampshire high school—the "gay students" and the "Rednecks." Tensions escalated between the groups when the Rednecks began occasionally giving the Nazi salute and a "Seig Heil" response when they encountered members of the gay student group. The gay group retaliated by wearing patches to school depicting the universal symbol for "no": a circle with the swastika in the middle and a diagonal line running through it. The principal was concerned about a further escalation of tension, which could have led to a disruption and banned the wearing of the patches as a violation of the school's dress code. A lawsuit was filed.

At trial, the court used *Johnson* to ascertain whether the patches were symbolic speech and whether, under *Tinker*, it was reasonable for school officials to conclude that the wearing of the patches might lead to material and substantial disruption of the school environment. The court concluded that the patches, although constituting speech, could be lawfully banned because of their potential for causing disruption.

Federal courts have often used *Spence* and *Johnson* to decide cases involving student speech and student dress. Both of these cases involve an analysis of symbolic expression to ascertain if it contains constitutional dimensions of speech. Although both occurred after *Tinker* and both arose out of nonschool criminal cases, *Spence* and *Johnson* have been added to the courts' toolbox of precedents that they use to decide disputes between schools and students about what students may say and wear while they are at school.

THE SUPREME COURT AND WHAT STUDENTS WEAR TO SCHOOL

The Supreme Court has issued four decisions on the free speech rights of students in the public schools and three non-education cases that lower courts often consult when deciding student speech cases. Taken together, the Supreme Court has fashioned, albeit in an ad hoc fashion, a discernible pathway for determining the constitutionality of school restrictions on students' dress. Supreme Court guidance can be summarized as follows:

- Symbolic expression is protected as pure free speech if it is intended to convey a particularized message and there is a high likelihood that those who view the message will understand the message. (*Tinker, Spence,* and *Johnson*)
- School regulations that pertain to student choice of attire must support an important or substantial governmental interest that is unrelated to the suppression of free expression, and any "incidental" restriction must be no greater than necessary to meet the governmental interest. (*O'Brien*)
- Schools may constitutionally regulate student expression that carries the imprimatur of the school so long as school authorities can articulate a legitimate pedagogical justification for their regulations. (*Hazelwood*)
- Schools can prohibit student dress that is lewd, indecent, or vulgar. (*Fraser*)
- Schools can ban student speech or attire that promotes illegal drug use. Such speech is not constitutionally protected in the school environment. (*Morse*)
- Schools can censor student speech that creates a material and substantial disruption, or that school officials reasonably anticipate

will create a material and substantial disruption, regardless of whether the speech can be banned under other constitutional guidelines. (*Tinker*)

These Supreme Court student-free-speech standards will assist readers in the following chapters.

[handwritten: diff to elementary school]

FREE SPEECH IN THE ELEMENTARY SCHOOLS

Tinker involved the speech of high school students. It found that students do not shed their constitutional rights at the schoolhouse gate. But do all students have the same degree of rights without regard to their age? The Supreme Court has not weighed in on this issue but several lower courts have. Below are the comments from several federal appellate courts:

- *Muller by Muller v. Jefferson Lighthouse School*, 98 F.3d 1530, 1539 (7th Cir. 1996)

  While eventually deciding whether a fourth grader could hand out invitations to a religious meeting based on a forum analysis rather than using *Tinker's* disruption standard, the Seventh Circuit concluded that "it is unlikely that *Tinker* and its progeny apply to public elementary (or preschool) students due to the importance age plays in student speech cases."

- *Walz v. Egg Harbor Township Board of Education*, 342 F.3d 271, 277 (3d Cir. 2003)

  A first-grade school student was denied permission to distribute gifts (candy canes) with religious messages at classroom holiday parties; however, he was allowed to distribute them outside the classroom. The court wrote about age and education in relation to free speech, stating, "As a general matter, the elementary school classroom, especially for kindergartners and first graders, is not a place for student advocacy." Furthermore, the court asserted, "the age of the students bears an important inverse relationship to the degree of control a school may exercise: as general matter, the younger the students, the more control a school may exercise."

- *S.G. v. Sayerville Board of Education*, 333 F.3d 417, 423 (3d Cir. 2003).

  "[A] school's authority to control student speech in an elementary school setting is undoubtedly greater than in a high school setting," according to the Third Circuit Court of Appeals.

> • *K.A. v. Pocono Mountain School District*, 710 F.3d 99, 111 (3d Cir. 2013).
>
>   The Third Circuit Court of Appeals affirmed the right of an elementary school student to distribute invitations to her classmates to a Christmas party at her church. The court recognized that *Tinker* does not "cabin" First Amendment Rights to older students. The panel wrote, we "hold that the *Tinker* analysis has sufficient flexibility to accommodate the educational, developmental, and disciplinary interests at play in the elementary school environment."
>
> None of these cases dealt specifically with dress codes or school uniforms. Nevertheless, these decisions indicate that a federal court might take a student's age into account when deciding a case about the constitutionality of a school regulation restricting student dress or requiring students to wear uniforms.

NOTES

1. Nate Hentoff, *Living the Bill of Rights: How to Be an Authentic American* (Berkeley, CA: University of California Press, 1998), 73.

2. Pugsley v. Sellmeyer, 250 S.W. 538, 539–40 (Ark. 1923).

3. Ibid., 539.

4. Ibid., 540.

5. Newton Edwards, "Legal Authority of Boards of Education to Enforce Rules and Regulations," 31 *Elementary School Journal* (1931): 446–59, 466.

6. State ex rel. Dresser v. District Board of School District No. 1 (St. Croix Falls), 135 Wis. 619, 628 (1908).

7. New Jersey v. T.L.O., 469 U.S. 525 (1985).

8. Goss v. Lopez, 419 U.S. 565 (1975).

9. Brown v. Board of Education, 347 U.S. 483 (1954).

10. 393 U.S. 503 (1969).

11. Bivens v. Albuquerque Public Schools, 899 F. Supp. 556, 559 (D.N.M. 1995).

12. David L. Hudson Jr., *The Silencing of Student Voices: Preserving Free Speech in America's Schools* (Nashville, TN: First Amendment Center, 2003), 6.

13. Palko v. Connecticut, 302 U.S. 319, 327 (1937).

14. *See, e.g.*, Texas v. Johnson, 491 U.S. 397 (1989 (burning the American flag as a protected form of speech).

15. United States v. Schwimmer, 279 U.S. 644, 654–55 (1929) (Holmes, J. dissenting).

16. Terminello v. Chicago, 337 U.S. 1, 4 (1949).

17. Chaplinsky v. New Hampshire, 315 U.S. 568 (1942).

18. Brandenburg v. Ohio, 395 U.S. 444 (1969).

19. Beauharnais v. Illinois, 343 U.S. 250 (1952).

20. New York v. Ferber, 458 U.S. 747 (1982).

21. Texas v. Johnson, 491 U.S. 397, 414 (1989).

22. Ward v. Rock Against Racism, 491 U.S. 781, 791 (1989).

23. 505 U.S. 377 (1992).

24. Palmer v. Waxahachie Independent School District, 579 F.3d 502 (5th Cir. 2009).

25. 393 U.S. 503 (1969).

26. Ibid., 507.

27. Ibid., 509.

28. Todd A. DeMitchell, Richard Fossey, & Casey Cobb, "Dress Codes in the Public Schools: Principals, Policies and Precepts. 29 *Journal of Law and Education* 31, 47 (2000).

29. *See* Ginsberg v. New York, 390 U.S. 629 (1968) (affirming the constitutionality of a New York criminal statute that prohibited the sale to minors of material defined to be obscene, because it was rational for the legislature to find that exposing minors to such material might be harmful even if such material would not be obscene to adults).

30. New Jersey v. T.L.O., 469 U.S. 325 (1985). "[S]tudents within the school environment have a lesser expectation of privacy than members of the population generally." Ibid., 348 (Powell, J. concurring).

31. Martha M. McCarthy, Nelda H. Cambron-McCabe, & Stephen B. Thomas, *Public School Law: Teachers' and Students' Rights* (Boston: Allyn and Bacon, 1998), 114–15.

32. Denno v. School Board of Volusia County, 959 F. Supp. 1481 (M.D. Fla. 1997).

33. Board of Education v. Pico, 457 U.S. 853, 869 (1982).

34. Bethel School District No. 403 v. Fraser, 478 U.S. at 681.

35. Ibid.

36. Ibid. Also *see*, Justice Black's dissent in the seminal student-free-speech case, Tinker v. Des Moines, 393 U.S. 503, 525 (1969) (Black, J. dissenting), lamenting in stinging words that the majority's decision "wholly without constitutional reasons . . . subjects all the public schools in this country to the whims and caprices of their loudest-mouthed, and maybe not their brightest, students."

37. Tinker v. Des Moines Independent School District, 393 U.S. 503 (1969).

38. Ibid., 511. For a picture of the Tinkers with their black armbands, see Hudson, *supra*, note 12 p. 12. It is interesting to note that in the picture of Mary Beth and John Tinker, their black armbands had a peace symbol on them; a fact not discussed in the case.

39. Ibid., 507.

40. Ibid., 511.

41. Ibid.

42. Ibid., 513.

43. Ibid., 508.

44. Ibid., 513.

45. Ibid., 508. The use of the second prong has been spotty. The Third Circuit Court of Appeals wrote, "The precise scope of Tinker's interference with the rights of others' language is unclear." Saxe v. State College Area School District, 240 F.3d 200, 217 (3d Cir. 2001).

46. Ibid., 513.

47. Bannister v. Paradis, 316 F. Supp. 185 (D.N.H. 1970).

48. For a contrary view on a school restriction against wearing blue jeans, *see* Fowler v. Williamson, 448 F. Supp. 497 (W.D.N.C. 1978) (school principal's prohibition against wearing blue jeans to graduation ceremony did not violate student's constitutional rights).

49. Bethel School District No. 403 v. Fraser, 478 U.S. 675, 687 (1986) (Brennan, J., concurring). The entire nominating speech follows:
"I know a man who is firm—he's firm in his pants, he's firm in his shirt, his character is firm—but most . . . of all, his belief in you, the students of Bethel, is firm."
"Jeff Kuhlman is a man who takes his point and pounds it in. If necessary, he'll take an issue and nail it to the wall. He doesn't attack things in spurts—he drives hard, pushing and pushing until finally—he succeeds."
"Jeff is a man who will go to the very end—even the climax, for each and every one of you."
"So vote for Jeff for A.S.B. vice-president—he'll never come between you and the best our high school can be." Ibid.

50. 478 U.S. 675 (1986).

51. Ibid., 678.

52. Ibid., 679.

53. Ibid., 682.

54. Ibid.

55. Bethel School District No. 403 v. Fraser, 478 U.S. at 682.

56. Ibid.

57. Ibid., 683.

58. Boroff v. Van Wert City Board of Education, 220 F.3d 465, 471 (6th Cir. 2000); *cert. denied* 532 U.S. 920 (2001).

59. 484 U.S. 260 (1988).

60. Ibid.

61. Ibid., 270.

62. Ibid., 271.

63. Ibid., 273.

64. Ibid., 267.

65. Ibid., 266 (quoting *Fraser*, 478 U.S. at 685).

66. 551 U.S. 393 (2007).

67. Frederick v. Morse, 2003 U.S. Dist. LEXIS 27270 (D. Alaska May 27, 2003).

68. Frederick v. Morse, 439 F.3d 1114 (9th Cir. 2006).

69. Morse v. Frederick, 551 U.S. 393 (2007).

70. If Frederick's words were meaningless, could they constitute speech? If they were not speech could his right to free speech be abridged when there was no speech? Do a string of words without communicative intent constitute speech?

71. 515 U.S. 646, 661 (1995) ("[d]eterring drug use by schoolchildren is an 'important—indeed, perhaps compelling interest").

72. 536 U.S. 822, 834 (2002). ("The drug abuse problem among our Nation's youth has hardly abated since *Vernonia* was decided in 1995. In fact, evidence suggests that it has only grown worse.") Ibid.

73. Ibid., 408.

74. Ibid.

75. Ibid., 410. *See* Justice Alito's concurrence: "The special characteristic that is relevant in this case is the threat to the physical safety of students. . . . Students may be compelled on a daily basis to spend time at close quarters with other students who may do them harm. Experience shows that schools can be places of special danger." Ibid., 424 (Alito, J., concurring).

76. Ibid., 409–10.

77. For example *see*, David Schimmel, "*Morse v. Frederick*: Did the Supreme Court Weaken or Strengthen Student Freedom of Expression?" 226, *Education Law Reporter* 557 (2008); Kathleen Conn, "The Long and the Short of the Public School's Disciplinary Arm: Will *Morse v. Frederick* Make a Difference?" 227, *Education Law Reporter* 1 (2008).

78. Bob Kennedy, *Morse v. Frederick*: The Supreme Court Just Says No to "Bong Hits 4 Jesus," 20, *Education Law* 5, 6 (2007) (North Carolina Bar Association, Education Law Section). Available at https://educationlaw.ncbar.org/media/974994/10_2007.pdf.

79. Tinker v. Des Moines School District, 393 U.S. at 505.

80. 391 U.S. 367 (1968).

81. Ibid., 376.

82. Ibid.

83. Ibid., 377.

84. *See e.g.*, Palmer v. Waxahachie Independent School District, 579 F.3d 502 (5th Cir. 2009); Jacobs v. Clark County School District, 526 F.3d 419 (9th Cir. 2008); Blau v. Fort Thomas Public School District, 401 F.3d 381 (6th Cir. 2005).

85. Long v Board of Education of Jefferson County, 121 F. Supp. 2d 621 (W.D. Ky. (2000); affrm'd 2001 U.S. App. Lexis 18103 (6th Cir. 2001).

86. Ibid.

87. Ibid., 626.

88. Ibid.

89. 418 U.S. 405 (1974).

90. Three Seattle police officers observed the flag from the street. The officers arrested the owner with no disruption or altercation. There was no evidence that the flag

attracted any attention on the street, nor did Spence do anything to draw attention to the flag. Ibid., 406–9.

91. Ibid. 410–11.

92. Ibid., 415 n. 8.

93. Ibid., 410.

94. Ibid. citing West Virginia State Board of Education, 319 U.S. at 632.

95. Ibid., 411.

96. 40 F. Supp. 2d 335 (D. Md. 1997).

97. 491 U.S. 397 (1989).

98. Ibid., 399. The protestors chanted, while the flag burned, "America, the red, white, and blue, we spit on you." Ibid.

99. Ibid., 406.

100. Ibid., 407.

101. Ibid., 417.

102. Ibid., 419. The Court concluded, "We do not consecrate the flag by punishing its desecration, for in doing so we dilute the freedom that this cherished symbol represents." Ibid., 420.

103. Ibid., 414.

104. Ibid., 404.

105. 421 F. Supp. 2d 410 (D.N.H. 2006).

THREE

Dress Codes

Pants, Hats, and Gangs — The Clothes Are the Message

The very nature of public education requires limitations on one's personal liberty in order for the learning process to proceed.
                                        —*Richards v. Thurston*[1]

In the last chapter, we reviewed the U.S. Supreme Court's decisions about the free speech rights of students. As we have seen, the Court has placed constitutional limitations on the authority of school officials to censor students' speech while they are at school—although officials can certainly ban disruptive speech and lewd speech and speech that celebrates or promotes illegal drug use or other illegal behavior. School authorities can also censor student speech that carries the imprimatur of the school. We also reviewed the Supreme Court's leading non-education cases that provide an emerging standard for judging the constitutionality of school rules governing student clothing.

In spite of the articulation of these various free speech tests, it is noteworthy that the United States Supreme Court has not decided any cases involving student attire, refusing to review lower court decisions on the subject. Therefore, guidance for navigating the course between protecting students' constitutional rights and providing an environment conducive to student learning and student safety is left to the lower courts. Frequently, the lack of guidance from the Supreme Court has led to conflicting decisions, with constitutional rights being defined differently from one federal circuit to the next.

up to lower courts which has lead to lack of clarity

31

NON-SPECIFIC STUDENT MESSAGES

Over the years, students have filed numerous lawsuits challenging school bans on specific messages conveyed on student clothing. As we will see in the next two chapters, students have claimed a right to proclaim messages on their clothing that state their opposition to abortion, their loyalty to the antebellum South, their attitudes about drugs, their positions on homosexuality, and a variety of other social and political issues.

But students have also filed lawsuits in which they have claimed a First Amendment right to wear clothing that conveys no textual or graphic message, and it is these cases that we will examine in this chapter. In essence, students in these cases argued that their clothing choices were expressions of their individuality, their personal tastes, their personalities, or their affiliation with a particular ethnic group; and that these expressions are protected under the Free Speech clause of the First Amendment.

In deciding the cases discussed in this chapter, the courts often looked to Supreme Court decisions that spelled out when an individual's conduct has some expressive element that entitles it to First Amendment protection. The Supreme Court has made clear that not all expressive conduct is protected by the First Amendment. To bring a free speech claim based on conduct and not words, claimants must pass a two-part test discussed in the previous chapter. First, they must show that their conduct "conveys a particularized message." And second, they must show that there is a great likelihood that those who view it will understand the message.[2]

CLOTHING AS A SYMBOL

In chapter 2, we discussed the Supreme Court cases on symbolic speech, starting with the seminal case of *Tinker v. Des Moines Independent Community School District*,[3] in which the court ruled that a black armband worn in protest of the war in Vietnam was "akin to pure speech." Furthermore, in two non-education cases (*Texas v. Johnson*[4] and *Spence v. Washington*[5]), the Supreme Court articulated standards for determining when nonverbal activities (burning an American flag, for example) contain an expressive element that entitles the activity to constitutional protection under the First Amendment. Lower courts have drawn on these Supreme Court precedents in deciding cases brought by students who claim a First Amendment right to wear clothing that arguably conveys some constitutionally protected message even though the clothing bears no textual message.

Bivens v. Albuquerque Public Schools: *The Case of the Sagging Pants*

We begin our review of cases by looking at *Bivens v. Albuquerque Public Schools*.[6] In this case, Richard Bivens, a ninth grader at Albuquerque's Del Norte High School, received a long-term suspension after he repeatedly refused to comply with his school's dress code, which prohibited students from wearing sagging pants. The school district maintained that its prohibition against sagging pants was justified since the wearing of sagging pants was associated with gang activity. *sagging pants = gang*

Bivens sued the Albuquerque school system, arguing that he was not associated with a gang and that the pants reflected his identification and link with his black identity, black culture, and the styles of black urban youth. More specifically, Bivens maintained that wearing sagging pants "is part of a style known as 'hip hop,' whose roots are African American, and it represents a fashion statement for blacks and Hispanics extensively."[7]

A federal trial court acknowledged that some types of expressive conduct enjoy constitutional protection, such as the Tinker children's black armbands. Nevertheless, the court asserted, "[n]ot every defiant act by a high school student is constitutionally protected speech."[8] While public school students enjoy some degree of freedom of speech within the schoolhouse gates, it is balanced against the need to foster an educational atmosphere free from undue disruptions. *important 2*

In order to be entitled to constitutional protection, the *Bivens* court reasoned, expressive conduct must pass the two-part test devised by *Texas v. Johnson*, discussed in chapter 2. "First, the actor must intend to convey a particularized message, and second, there must be some likelihood that the message would be understood by those who observe the conduct."[9]

Granting that Bivens met the first prong of intentionality, the court was unpersuaded that Bivens could prevail on the record before the court on the second prong, requiring a showing that people who saw Bivens wearing sagging pants would understand that his clothing conveyed an expressive message. In the court's opinion, Bivens's sagging pants failed the second part of the two-part test. Whatever message Bivens intended to convey by wearing sagging pants was not readily apparent to those who saw his pants sag, the court concluded. If sagging is just a fashion trend of adolescents, then it would be devoid of a particularized message that would have the likelihood of being understood by others who saw the sagging pants. Therefore Bivens's First Amendment claim failed.

Bivens also raised a second constitutional argument—that the school district's dress code was unconstitutionally vague and did not give him fair notice of the type of clothing that was prohibited. The court rejected this argument as well. "I reject the notion that a school dress code prohibiting sagging must be expressed in inches or millimeters, any more than other styles prohibited by the dress code must be quantified exactly," the court ruled. The court noted that the dress code also prohibited "short shirts," "half-shirts," and "inappropriate tank tops" without stating precisely what those terms meant. The court saw no constitutional infirmity on a vagueness ground, concluding that "[t]he need to maintain appropriate discipline in schools must favor more administrative discretion than might be permitted in other parts of society." [10]

Isaacs v. Board of Education of Howard County: *Headwraps*

Other students have claimed a broad constitutional right to choose their school clothing similar to the right Bivens unsuccessfully asserted. In *Isaacs v. Board of Education of Howard County*, Shermia Isaacs, a ninth grader in a Maryland high school, sued her school district after the assistant principal prohibited her from wearing a multicolored headwrap to school on the grounds that the headwrap violated the school's "no hats" policy. [11]

In considering Shermia's claims, a federal trial court first applied the same two-part test that another federal court had utilized in the *Bivens* case. Did Shermia intend to convey a particularized message when she wore her headwrap to school? And if so, would that message be generally understood by those who viewed it? This is essentially the test articulated by the Supreme Court in *Spence* and *Johnson*.

Shermia admitted that she occasionally wore the headwrap to school for the purpose of covering her hair when she was not satisfied with its appearance. Nevertheless, she and her mother maintained that Shermia's primary motivation for wearing the headwrap was to say symbolically "I celebrate my African-American and Jamaican heritage." [12]

The court was not entirely satisfied that Shermia's headwrap met either parts of the two-part test, but the court concluded that the headwrap did constitute symbolic speech. Even so, the court noted, the school district's prohibition against Shermia's headwrap would be upheld if the school's "no hats" policy furthered an important governmental interest.

In the court's view, the school district had articulated an important governmental interest in enforcing its policy, which was to provide "a safe, respectful school environment that is conducive to education and learning." [13]

The court spelled out the ways in which the school district's governmental interests were furthered by the "no hats" rule:

> [H]ats can (i) cause increased horseplay and conflict in the hallways, (ii) obscure the teacher's view of the student wearing the hat or view of the students sitting behind that student (and as a result can cause the teacher to miss signs of substance abuse or other health problems), (iii) obscure students' view of the blackboard, (iv) allow students to hide

contraband, and (v) foster a less respectful and focused climate of learning."[14]

The court found the school district's justifications for its "no hats" rule to be valid and not irrational or arbitrary, as Shermia contended. Furthermore, the court said it was abundantly clear that the school district enforced its "no hats" rule for reasons unrelated to the suppression of free expression. In the court's view, the rule's restriction on expression was no greater than necessary to further the school's interests. Finally, the court pointed out that Shermia had alternate means of expressing her message within the school's dress code, including the wearing of traditional African dress or jewelry to class.

Shermia also argued that the school's refusal to allow her to wear a headwrap to school violated her constitutional right to be secure in her person. In support of that argument she cited a decision by the Fourth Circuit Court of Appeals that had found "that a person's right to wear his hair as he wishes is 'an aspect of the right to be secure in one's person guaranteed by the due process clause.'"[15]

Responding to this creative argument, the court pointed out that there were evident distinctions between hairstyle and clothing:

> Clearly . . . a public school's restrictions on headgear are far less intrusive on this personal freedom than similar restrictions on hairstyle. Headgear, like other clothing and unlike hair, is easily removed and replaced. Shermia is free to wear her headwrap outside of school and, apparently, is even free to wear the headwrap to and from school. The rule simply requires that she leaves the headwrap in her locker during the school day.[16]

In any event, the court went on, a determination that Shermia's desire to wear a particular headgear is entitled to some constitutional protection would not end the constitutional inquiry. "Personal freedoms are not absolute; they must yield when they intrude upon the freedom of others."[17] In the court's opinion, "[t]he reasons advanced by the school system for its 'no hat' restriction sufficiently and reasonably establish the need for the restriction's relatively minor infringement on personal freedom."[18]

Furthermore, Shermia's argument that allowing religious headgear undermined the content-neutral regulation also did not prevail. The court asserted that as a threshold matter, religious headgear is not symbolic speech. Instead "it is worn not to express a message to others but because of a mandate derived from a doctrine of reverence for a deity."[19] Even assuming that religious headgear is symbolic speech, it would receive increased constitutional protection because it implicated more than one constitutional right and would thus be considered as deserving hybrid constitutional protection for free speech and free expression.

In the court's view, the relative likelihood of disruption was great enough to justify the school system's "no hat" rule. "Furthermore," the court concluded, "it would be entirely unrealistic to ask school administrators . . . to decide on a hat-by-hat basis whether a particular hat poses sufficient danger of disruption."[20] Indeed, in the court's opinion, Shermia's argument that the school should be required to make administrative decisions about individual hats was unreasonable.

Grzywna v. Schenectady Central School District: A Red, White, and Blue Necklace

In *Grzywna v. Schenectady Central School District*, a mother sued the school district where her twelve-year-old daughter (known only as Jane Doe) attended school, claiming the district had violated her daughter's First Amendment rights by prohibiting her from wearing a homemade red, white, and blue beaded necklace.[21] According to the mother, her daughter wore the necklace "to show her support for the soldiers serving in Iraq (including certain members of her family) and to demonstrate her love of country."[22] School officials justified the ban on the grounds that the necklace was considered gang related and that school policy prohibited the wearing of gang-related items at school.

The school district responded to Grzywna's suit by filing a motion to dismiss. School authorities argued that wearing the necklace to school was not constitutionally protected since wearing the necklace conveyed no particularized message, and it was unlikely that anyone seeing Jane Doe wearing the necklace would understand that she was communicating a message. The school district also rejected the mother's argument that its dress code was unconstitutionally vague.

A federal trial court denied the school district's dismissal motion without giving much of an indication about how it might ultimately rule in the case. The court concluded that it could not be said with certainty in the early phase of the lawsuit whether Jane Doe had a constitutional right to wear the necklace. Jane herself maintained that wearing the necklace conveyed a particularized expressive message, and the court determined that it could not be said for certain that viewers would fail to understand that message.

> [I]t cannot be questioned [the court wrote] that Plaintiff's wearing of the red, white and blue necklace coincided with the ongoing war in Iraq and that there is public debate about that war. While plaintiff claims that she was showing support for her country, for her family members who served in Iraq, and for her support of members of the military in general, people do not automatically associate the colors red, white and blue (or a red, white, and blue beaded necklace) as necessarily demonstrating support for the troops.[23]

Thus, the court concluded that it was simply unclear at the early stage of the litigation "whether anything about the necklace itself or the context in which Plaintiff wore the necklace gave any particular meaning to it."[24] Merely intending to express an idea is not sufficient for the conduct to be considered speech. The court also declined to rule definitively on Jane Doe's claim that the school district's student dress policy was unconstitutionally vague.

WEARING WHAT I LIKE TO SCHOOL

Bannister v. Paradis: *A Constitutional Right to Wear Blue Jeans to School?*

In *Bannister v. Paradis*, an old federal court case out of New Hampshire, a federal court was asked to decide on the constitutionality of a school board policy that prohibited students from wearing "dungarees" to school.[25] Kevin Bannister, a sixth grader, wore blue jeans to school in violation of the "no dungarees" rule and was sent home.

Antonio Paradis, the school principal, defended the school district's dress code in court. As summarized by the court,

> [Paridis] testified that discipline in school is essential to the educational process, and that proper dress is a part of a good educational climate. It was his opinion that if students wear working or play clothes to school, it leads to a relaxed attitude and such an attitude detracts from discipline and a proper educational climate. Mr. Paradis stated further that students with patches on their clothes and students with dirty clothes, regardless of the type of clothing, should be sent home.[26]

Principal Paradis's testimony was supplemented by the school board chairman, an airline pilot. The chairman asserted, "California students had poor academic records and that this was due to the sloppy and casual attire worn by them to school."[27] As the trial court pointed out, the chairman did not provide any basis for claiming that California students had poor academic records.

In a 1970 decision that perhaps reflected the expansive spirit of the 1970s regarding students' constitutional rights, a federal trial judge expressed no patience with the school board's dress code. "There is no evidence that the wearing of dungarees of any color had ever caused any disturbance at the school or given rise to any disciplinary problems," the court observed. "Kevin's wearing of blue jeans did not cause any disturbance and there was no disciplinary problem involved except the one involving Kevin himself." Thus, the court stated, "It can be fairly concluded that wearing clean blue jeans does not constitute a danger to the health or safety of other pupils and that wearing them does not disrupt the other pupils."[28]

The judge in the case was bound by a First Circuit decision that had recognized a constitutional right of a student to choose the length of his hair. Based on the language of that opinion, the court concluded "a person's right to wear clothes of his own choosing provided that, in the case of a schoolboy, they are neat and clean, is a constitutional right protected and guaranteed by the Fourteenth Amendment."[29]

The court acknowledged that the right to wear blue jeans to school did not rank very high on "the scale of values of constitutional liberties."[30] Nevertheless, in the court's view, the school had not been able to show that the wearing of blue jeans "inhibited or tended to inhibit the educational process."[31] Thus, the court ruled in Kevin's favor, finding "that the defendants have not justified the intrusion on the personal liberty of Kevin Bannister, small as that intrusion may be, and that the prohibition against wearing dungarees is unconstitutional and invalid."[32] The court concluded by enjoining the school district from enforcing its rule against students wearing dungarees to school.

Although the court struck down the school district's ban on blue jeans, it did not prohibit all school restrictions on student clothing. Specifically, the court said this:

> We realize that a school can, and must, for its own preservation exclude persons who are unsanitary, obscenely or scantily clad. Good hygiene and the health of the other pupils require that dirty clothes of any nature, whether they be dress clothes or dungarees, should be prohibited. Nor does the Court see anything unconstitutional in a school board prohibiting scantily clad students because it is obvious that the lack of proper covering, particularly with female students, might tend to distract other pupils and be disruptive of the educational process and school discipline.[33]

It should be remembered that the *Paradis* case was decided before the Supreme Court decisions discussed in the last chapter that laid out a two-part test for determining when an individual's conduct has an expressive element that entitles it to constitutional protection. Specifically, the *Paradis* court did not ask whether Kevin Bannister was conveying a "particularized message" by wearing blue jeans or whether people seeing him wear the jeans would understand that he was engaged in expression simply because he was wearing jeans.

Blau v. Fort Thomas Public School District: *Do Parents Have the Right to Decide What Their Children Wear to School?*

We conclude our review of broad dress-code challenges with an analysis of *Blau v. Fort Thomas Public School District*, a 2005 decision by the Sixth Circuit Court of Appeals.[34] Robert Blau, a lawyer and parent of Amanda Blau, sued Fort Thomas Public School District, claiming the dress code at his daughter's middle school violated Amanda's constitutional rights and his constitutional rights as Amanda's father. Blau raised three constitutional challenges: 1) the dress code violated Amanda's First Amendment right to free expression; 2) the code violated Amanda's substantive due-process right to wear the clothes of her own choosing; and 3) the code violated Blau's substantive due-process right to direct the upbringing of his child, including the control his child's dress.

The dress code had been developed by the middle school's Site Based Decision Making Council, which consisted of two parents, three teachers, and the principal. Although the code was not as restrictive as a school uniform code, it contained a number of detailed restrictions on student dress, which were summarized by the court:

- clothing that is too tight, revealing, or baggy as well as tops and bottoms that do not "overlap";
- "hats, caps, scarves, or sweatbands" except on "special event days" such as "spirit" or "reward" days;
- non-jewelry chains and chain wallets;
- clothing that is "distressed" or has "holes in it";
- "visible body piercing (other than ears)";
- "unnaturally colored hair that is distracting to the educational process," including "blue, green, red, purple [or] orange" hair;
- "clothing that is too long, flip-flop sandals, or high platform shoes";
- pants, shorts or skirts that are not of "a solid color of navy blue, black , any shade of khaki, or white";
- "shorts, skirts, or skorts "that do not "reach mid-thigh or longer";
- "bottoms made with stretch knits, flannel, or fleece such as sweatpants, jogging pants, or any type of athletic clothing" as well as "baggy, sagging, or form-fitting pants";
- tops that are not "a solid color" and are not "crew neck [style], polo style with buttons, oxford style, or turtleneck";
- tops with writing on them and "logos larger than the size of a 'quarter'. . . except 'Highlands' logos or other 'Highlands Spirit Wear'";
- tops that are not "of an appropriate size and fit"; and
- "form-fitting or baggy shirts" or "any material that is sheer or lightweight enough to be seen through."[35]

After Blau filed the lawsuit, the council modified the dress code, making it less restrictive in some ways but more restrictive in others. The modified code prohibited blue jeans as well as tops with plunging or revealing necklines; and it added a provision prohibiting any clothing that promoted drugs, alcohol, tobacco, or sex or that displayed offensive or degrading images. The modified code liberalized the restrictions on pants, skirts, and shorts—permitting any color; and it permitted striped or patterned tops.

In bringing the lawsuit, Amanda did not claim a desire to communicate a particular message through her clothing. Rather, she said, "she want[ed] to be able to wear clothes that 'look[ed] nice on [her],' that she 'feels good in' and that express her individuality."[36] Nor had she sued on religious grounds. Neither Amanda nor her father claimed the code was incompatible with their religious beliefs. The father's chief complaint, as well, was that the dress code inhibited his daughter's "ability to wear clothing that she likes."[37]

A trial court dismissed the lawsuit on the school district's motion for summary judgment, finding no constitutional violations in the school district's dress code. The Blaus appealed to the Sixth Circuit Court of Appeals, which affirmed the trial court's dismissal.

The Sixth Circuit began its legal analysis by stating flatly that the school district had the authority to enforce its dress code under Sixth Circuit's own precedent. In a 2000 decision, the court had said that a school district could enforce a dress code that banned "offensive illustrations" by banning a student from wearing a nihilistic Marilyn Manson T-shirt.[38] Thus, "it surely follows that a school district may enforce a dress code that regulates the types of pants and tops students may wear and may do so with respect to a student who does not wish to convey 'any particular message' through her clothing but simply wants to wear clothes that 'look nice' on her."[39]

The Sixth Circuit then went on to ask a more basic question: Does the First Amendment cover a claim such as Amanda's at all? "The protections of the First Amendment do not generally apply to conduct in and of itself," the court pointed out.[40] "To bring a free-speech claim regarding actions rather than word, claimants must show that their conduct 'conveys a particularized message' and 'the likelihood [is] great that the message [will] be understood by those who view[ed] it."[41]

In the Sixth Circuit's view, the Blaus' complaints against the dress code at Amanda's school did not give rise to a constitutional claim because they had not met the burden of showing that the First Amendment protected Amanda's conduct, "which in this instance amounts to nothing more than a generalized and vague desire to express her middle-school individuality." As the Sixth Circuit explained, the First Amendment simply does not protect Amanda's "vague and attenuated notions of expression—namely, self-expression through any and all clothing that a 12-year-old may wish to wear on a given day."[42]

The Blaus also argued that the school dress code was constitutionally overbroad because it suppressed a substantial amount of protected conduct that other students might engage in. But the Sixth Circuit rejected this claim as well. Courts will sustain a governmental regulation that restricts expressive conduct, the Sixth Circuit pointed out, relying on *Spence* and *Johnson*, if (1) the regulation was adopted for reasons not related to the suppression of expression, (2) the regulation furthers an important or substantial governmental interest, and (3) the regulation does not burden expression more than necessary to further the governmental interest.

In the Sixth Circuit's view, the dress code at Amanda's school passed constitutional muster. Contrary to the Blaus' assertions, the court concluded that the code had not been adopted for the purpose of suppressing speech. Rather, the school's Site Based Decision Making Council had adopted the code to enhance school safety, improve the learning environment, promote good behavior, enhance students' self-esteem, bridge socioeconomic differences between families, and reduce the clothing costs for families. In the court's view, these were important governmental interests.

Furthermore, the Sixth Circuit was convinced that the school's dress code did not suppress more expressive conduct than was necessary to further its interests. The code only restricted students' dress during school hours, so students were free to wear what they wished in the evenings and on weekends. In addition, the school offered adequate alternative outlets of expression. For example, the court noted, students could write for the school newspaper, participate in extracurricular activities, and wear buttons expressing their viewpoints.

Having disposed of the Blaus' First Amendment claims, the court next turned to Amanda's claim that the dress code violated her substantive due process rights under the Fourteenth Amendment. The court quickly dismissed this claim as well, pointing out that the dress code clearly had a rational basis and Amanda's asserted right to wear what she wanted to school was not a fundamental constitutional right that would require stricter judicial scrutiny.

Finally, the court considered Robert Blau's interesting argument that the dress code violated his substantive due process right to control the upbringing of Amanda, which included a constitutional right to choose her clothing. Blau based this argument on two Supreme Court cases, both decided in the 1920s, which had recognized the constitutional right of parents to direct the education of their children.[43]

The Sixth Circuit rejected this argument, emphatically ruling that the holdings in these old cases could not be stretched to include the constitutional right of parents to exempt their children from school dress codes. "While parents may have a fundamental right to decide *whether* to send their child to a public school," the court emphasized, "they do not have a fundamental right generally to direct *how* a public school teaches their child."[44] On the contrary, "[w]hether it is the school curriculum, the hours of the school day, school discipline, the timing and content of examinations, the individuals hired to teach at the school, the extracurricular activities offered at the school, or, as here, a dress code, these issues of public education are generally committed to the control of state and local authorities."[45]

Blau v. Fort Thomas Public School District is a particularly important case for two reasons. First, contrary to most of the cases we reviewed in this chapter, *Blau* is a federal court case decided at the appellate level. Although the Sixth Circuit Court's opinion is binding precedent only within the boundaries of the Sixth Circuit (the states of Kentucky, Ohio, and Tennessee), it may be persuasive in other federal circuits when they consider student free speech issues.

In addition, the *Blau* decision is important because the court considered a broad range of constitutional challenges against a school dress code, including the argument that parents have a substantive due process right to control the dress of their children while at school. Indeed, it is hard to imagine any new constitutional theory that could be presented to defeat a school's dress code beyond the ones raised by Robert Blau and his daughter.

Thus, from the perspective of school districts and school leaders, the *Blau* decision is a particularly good decision. Regardless of the constitutional theory that a parent may utilize to defeat a dress code, it is likely that the Sixth Circuit has already examined that theory and rejected it.

Bell v. Anderson Community Schools: *An Objection to Bland Clothing*

In *Bell v. Anderson Community School*, an unpublished case decided in 2007, a federal trial court in Indiana relied heavily on the Sixth Circuit's *Blau* opinion to reject a constitutional attack on a school district's dress code.[46] The Anderson Community Schools adopted a dress code containing detailed restrictions on student dress, somewhat similar to those that were approved in *Blau*, including a requirement that students wear "pants, trousers, capris, skirts, skorts, or jumpers that are black, navy, or khaki colored."[47] The dress code did not require students to buy specific brands or styles of clothing or dictate the exact articles that students were required to buy.

Scott and Laura Bell, parents of five children who were enrolled in the school system, filed a lawsuit objecting to the code on constitutional grounds. They claimed they lacked the clothing the new code required and would have to buy a completely new wardrobe for each child. In addition, they complained "that being able to wear the clothes they want is fundamental to their children's 'freedom of speech, expression, and freedom of happiness.'"[48] Specifically, the Bells claimed that wearing the "bland colors" that the dress code proscribed would exacerbate their emotional issues as well as their depression. They also argued that their children should be free to choose clothing "best suited to their personality."[49]

The Bells had filed suit without an attorney, and the federal trial judge admitted having difficulty determining the legal theories under which they were proceeding. Nevertheless, the court denied their claims, relying heavily on the Sixth Circuit's *Blau* decision.

As we discussed above, in *Blau*, the Indiana court noted, the Sixth Circuit had ruled that the First Amendment did not protect a student's right "to wear whatever she desired" and upheld a school district's dress code against constitutional challenge. This set the stage for the Bells' trial.

The Indiana court found the *Blau* decision persuasive. "The Bells have not shown that their children wish to convey any particularized message at all," the court wrote. "They have only hinted that this Dress Code will affect their children's 'freedom of expression' and that wearing 'such bland colors will promote or increase their emotional disorders as well as depression.'"[50] The First Amendment does not protect such vague and attenuated notions of expression, the court ruled.

Another case that also found the *Blau* position persuasive regarding "vague and attenuated notions of self-expression through clothing" is *Bar-Navon v. Brevard County School Board.*[51] In an unpublished opinion, the Eleventh Circuit Court of Appeals upheld a dress code that set out this standard:

> Pierced jewelry shall be limited to the ear. Dog collars, tongue rings, wallet chains, large hair picks, chains that connect one part of the body to another, or jewelry/accessories that pose a safety concern for the student or others shall be prohibited.[52]

Danielle, then a 16-year-old tenth-grade student at Viera High School, had piercings located on her tongue, nasal septum, lip, navel, and chest. She brought suit when she was suspended and prohibited from wearing the pierced jewelry. She did not intend to make a political or religious statement with her piercings. However, she asserted that her piercings were an expression of her "individuality," "non-conformity and wild side," her "openness" to new ideas, and her "readiness to take on challenges in life."[53] In other words, she wanted to wear what she wanted to wear to school.

While noting that students enjoy some measure of the constitutional right to free speech within the special characteristics of the public school environment, the Eleventh Circuit ruled that Danielle carried the burden of showing she had a protected expressive right to wear jewelry that communicated her individuality. Citing *Spence* and *Johnson*, the Court of Appeals questioned whether the piercings implicated free speech protection of the First Amendment. However, setting aside its skepticism, the court assumed some measure of communication in the piercings, and analyzed the school's dress code by applying an intermediate level of scrutiny to determine the code's constitutionality.

The dress code, the Eleventh Circuit Court of Appeals asserted, furthered legitimate educational objectives. "The School Board sought to avoid extreme dress or appearance which might create a school disturbance or which could be hazardous to the students or others."[54] The court concluded the jewelry limitation was narrowly tailored and there were ample alternatives for student speech.

GANGS AND GANG ATTIRE

Dress codes have often targeted gangs in the schools. In some instances, dress codes contain explicit prohibitions against gang clothing, and these prohibitions have been challenged more than once in federal courts on First Amendment grounds.

A major legal question pertaining to gang-related dress codes is whether they violate the substantive due process rights of students. Under the Fourteenth Amendment, public schools may not adopt rules or regulations that violate the substantive due process rights of their students. An important aspect of substantive due process is vagueness. The void for vagueness doctrine of the Fourteenth Amendment prevents arbitrary and discriminatory enforcement of statutes and regulations.[55] A regulation or statute is void on its face when it is so vague that persons of common intelligence must necessarily guess at its meaning and its application.[56]

In other words, a regulation or policy violates due process guarantees if a reasonable person would not know what to refrain from doing or what must be done in order to follow the law, rule, or regulation. If the rule is vague it does not provide fair notice or warning. A second substantive due process consideration is whether a regulation or policy is constitutionally overbroad because it prohibits constitutionally protected activity.[57] Comporting with the requirements of substantive due process can be a challenge for gang-related dress codes.

The Rosary and Gang Identification

An example of a gang-related dress-code policy that ran afoul of substantive due process is in the one that was litigated in a case against New Caney High School in Montgomery County, Texas. The policy prohibited gang-related attire in school or at school-related events. In enforcing this policy, school officials prohibited students from wearing rosaries outside of their clothing on the grounds that rosaries were considered to be gang-related apparel. Rosaries were not specifically listed as gang apparel in the policy.[58] However, a police officer, the Gang-Liaison Officer, identified gang members of the United Homies as wearing rosaries within the area of the school district. Even though school authorities stated that two students who wore rosaries to school for several months were not members of a gang (nor were they ever misidentified as gang members[59]) were told that for their safety they could not wear their rosaries outside of their shirts while at school. The students brought suit in federal district court.

In *Chalifoux v. New Caney Independent School District*, a federal court ruled that the school district's gang-related clothing policy violated substantive due process on the grounds that it was unconstitutionally vague. The policy lacked specific definition for gang apparel and thus did not provide adequate notice of what clothing was prohibited, and it "provided excessive discretion to law enforcement officials in defining the parameters of its ban on gang-related apparel."[60] The school's definition, the court asserted, revealed little about what apparel was considered prohibited.

Without a definition, students were not on notice that the wearing of a rosary on the outside of the shirt was prohibited. In addition, the gang-related dress code placed too much discretion on local officials as to what kind of apparel was considered gang-related and thus was susceptible to being banned.

Moreover, the court found that the policy infringed on First Amendment rights of speech and a sincere expression of religious beliefs. Not all gang members wore rosaries and not all individuals who wore rosaries were gang members.

yes

The Cross Tattoo

Brianna Stephenson, as an eighth grader, tattooed a small cross between her thumb and index finger. The cross was not intended as a religious symbol. It was also not intended as gang identification. Brianna did not have a record of disciplinary problems; in fact she was considered by her teachers to be conscientious and diligent. Despite having a learning disability, she made the honor role. She wore the cross tattoo without incident for thirty months. That changed when her high school, West High School, experienced an increase in gang activity with associated violence and intimidation.

In response to the gang problem, school officials developed a policy entitled "Proactive Disciplinary Position K–12." The policy stated, in pertinent part, that "[g]ang related activities such as display of 'colors,' symbols, signals, signs, etc., will not be tolerated on school grounds."

Soon after the policy was implemented, a school counselor with whom Brianna was meeting saw the tattoo and informed the associate principal. It was determined that the tattoo of the cross was a gang symbol even though there was no evidence that Brianna was involved in gang activity and no other student filed a complaint about her tattoo being a gang symbol. Brianna was suspended for one day. In the subsequent meeting with Brianna and her parents, the associate principal informed them that Brianna had to either remove or alter the tattoo or face a ten-day suspension.

Brianna, concerned that altering the tattoo would make it bigger and that school authorities and others might consider the alteration to be a gang symbol, decided to undergo laser treatment to remove the tattoo, leaving a scar in place of the tattoo. Brianna brought suit following the removal of the tattoo, arguing in part that the gang-related policy violated her right to due process because the policy was void for vagueness.

The case, *Stephenson v. Davenport Community School District*, wound its way to the federal Court of Appeals for the Eighth Circuit.[61] The appellate court held that the policy was void for vagueness. The fact that the term "gang" had not been defined rendered the policy defective. The court asserted that without a definition of gang, the colors, symbols, signals, and signs that were prohibited by the policy had no central definition to which colors, symbols, signals, and signs could be applied.

If the school district desired to draft a policy prohibiting students from wearing apparel affiliated with gangs, the court instructed, it must "define with some care" the "gang related activities" it wished students to avoid.[62] In its present form, the court ruled, "the District regulation violates the central purposes of the vagueness doctrine because it fails to provide adequate notice regarding unacceptable conduct and fails to offer clear guidance for those who apply it. A person of common intelligence must necessarily guess at the undefined meaning of 'gang related activities.'"[63]

In addition, as in *Chalifoux*, discussed above, the policy provided virtually unfettered discretion for school authorities and police officers to define gang-related activity and symbols in any way they chose.[64] Because the term lacked a working definition it failed to provide meaningful guidance for educators who were charged with enforcing the policy.

Gangs and Sports Teams

Jeglin v. San Jacinto Unified School District considered whether a California school district could pass a rule prohibiting students from wearing clothing that bore "writing, pictures, or any other insignia which identifies any professional sports team or college on school district campuses or at school district functions."[65] The school district adopted the policy to curtail gang activity and applied it to all school campuses, including the high school, middle school, and the district's four elementary schools. Several students challenged the policy. For example, Marvin Jeglin wore a Chicago Bears professional team jacket to the middle school; Ariel Jeglin wore a blue sweatshirt identifying the University of California, Los Angeles, to her elementary school; and Darcee Le Borgne wore a University of San Diego sweatshirt to the high school. All were told their clothing violated the school district's dress code and that they would be disciplined if they disregarded the school district's policy against wearing clothing that displayed an affiliation with a college, a university, or a professional sports team.

The students sued, claiming a violation of their First Amendment rights, and a federal trial court applied the *Tinker* standard to the undisputed facts of the case. Under *Tinker* and binding precedent in the Ninth Circuit Court of Appeals, the court said, it was clear that public school students have a right to freedom of speech, which is not shed at the schoolhouse gates. In the court's view, this right "encompasses the wearing of clothing that displays a student's support of a college or university or professional sports team."[66]

However, "[t]he interest of the state in the maintenance of its education system is a compelling one and provokes a balancing of First Amendment rights with the state's efforts to preserve and protect its educational process."[67] Therefore, the court continued, school officials can censor student speech if they reasonably forecast the speech will trigger a substantial disruption in the school environment.

In the case before the court, San Jacinto school officials argued that the school district's rule was justified because the wearing of clothing affiliated with a college or a sports team was linked to gang activity. The court considered the evidence of gang activity at all three school levels. Regarding the elementary schools, the court ruled that the school district had offered no evidence of gang presence in any of the district's four elementary schools. In the court's view, there was no justification for applying the school district's restrictive dress code to the elementary school population.

At the middle school level, the court found only negligible evidence of gang activity. Therefore, the court ruled that the school district's rule against clothing affiliated with athletic teams and colleges was an unwarranted infringement on the First Amendment rights of middle school students.

The court heard conflicting evidence regarding gang activity at San Jacinto High School. Several students testified that gang members did not wear clothing affiliated with sports teams or colleges to display their gang affiliations, but school authorities presented evidence to the contrary. In the end, the court concluded that the school district had carried its burden of showing a gang presence, "albeit of undefined size and composition,"[68] at the high school and a need to enforce its restrictive dress code at the high school level as a means of preventing possible disruption. Therefore, the court permitted the school district to enforce its dress policy at the high school level.

Jeglin v. San Jacinto Unified School District is somewhat difficult to categorize. It could be argued that the case is really about targeted student speech, since each of the students who sued had worn clothing to school that identified their affiliation with a particular sports team or college. On the other hand, it appears the students were motivated more by a desire to establish a broad constitutional right to choose their clothing rather than a drive to proclaim their allegiance to particular sports organizations.

Discussion: Dress Code Response to Gangs

School administrators have a legal and a professional duty to take reasonable steps to respond to violence associated with gang activity in the schools. The question is whether a dress code aimed at gang-related apparel is reasonable and workable. Given the susceptibility of such dress codes to fail the test of vagueness, are such codes workable? Can a gang-related dress code be drafted that will provide students with sufficient notice and definition of what is prohibited? Once a restriction is in place, many gangs morph their identifying symbols and signs for the specific purpose of keeping them secret from authorities, which may make a dress code that prohibits gang-related clothing ineffective.

The court in *Stephenson* captured this conundrum when it wrote, "Sadly, gang activity is not relegated to signs and symbols otherwise indecipherable to the uninitiated. In fact, gang symbols include common, seemingly benign jewelry, words and clothing."[69] Red and blue are colors of the Blood and Crips but they also the colors of the American flag.

Perhaps a better approach for combating gang activity is for school officials to focus energy and resources that will allow for an immediate response to any gang activity that endangers students or staff. Responding to violence or threats of violence is surely more important than focusing on clothing that may or may not be affiliated with gang behavior.

CONCLUSION

In this chapter, we looked at cases in which students challenged school dress codes on First Amendment grounds. In contrast to the cases discussed in the next two chapters, students in these cases did not claim a right to proclaim a specific textual or graphic message. Rather, they claimed a right to wear clothing that expressed their personality or their affiliation with a group or an ethnic or minority culture, or that, in one case, simply made the student feel good.

None of these cases ruled that school districts are prohibited by the First Amendment from imposing a dress code. Even in the case of *Bannister v. Paradis*, in which a court struck down a school dress code's ban on blue jeans, the decision affirmed a school district's right to impose a dress code to enforce standards of modesty and cleanliness. Cases in which students assert a constitutional right to wear whatever they want to school have met with little success. Unless the message is one that can be understood, the conduct cannot rise to the level of speech. In fact, the court in *Blau* raised the concern that elevating clothing to the level of constitutionally protected self-expression "would risk deprecating the First Amendment in cases in which a 'particularized message' does exist."[70]

Thus, as the cases discussed in this chapter illustrate, the courts often begin their analysis of whether a student's clothing choice is constitutionally protected by asking whether the clothing conveys a particularized message that others are likely to understand. Unless the answer to that question is affirmative, a court is unlikely to rule that a student's clothing choice is constitutionally protected.

Thus far, the Supreme Court has not decided the constitutionality of a student dress code as a general matter. In *Tinker*, the Court only considered the constitutionality a school rule that prohibited students from wearing black armbands, which the Court recognized as symbolic speech.

Nevertheless, the Supreme Court's *Tinker* decision recognized a constitutional distinction between a school's prohibition against a student's clearly expressive message such as the Tinker children's black armbands and a dress code intended to promote modesty or deportment. The Court pointed out that the *Tinker* case did "not relate to regulation of the length of skirts or the type of clothing, to hair style, or deportment," suggesting that general dress code regulations are constitutionally permissible.[71]

In the next two chapters, we will look at lawsuits brought by students who were barred from communicating targeted messages about a particular topic. Most of these cases involve printed text on T-shirts and sweat shirts.

NOTES

1. 424 F.2d 1281, 1285 (1st Cir. 1970).
2. Spence v. Washington, 418 U.S. 405, 411 (1974); Texas v. Johnson, 491 U.S. 397, 404 (1989).
3. 393 U.S. 503 (1969).
4. 491 U.S. 397 (1989).
5. 418 U.S. 405 (1974).
6. 899 F. Supp. 556 (D.N.M. 1995).
7. Ibid., 561. For a discussion of saggy pants as "a message of fashionable disobedience," see Onika K. Williams, "The Suppression of a Saggin' Expression: Exploring the 'Saggy Pants' style within a First Amendment Context," 85, *Indiana Law Journal* 1169, 1173 (2010) ("Wearing saggy pants should be viewed as an unconventional, expressive form of conduct that deserves First Amendment protection."). Ibid., 1172.
8. Ibid., 560.
9. Ibid., citing Texas v. Johnson, 491 U.S. 397, 404 (1989).
10. Ibid., 563.
11. 40 F. Supp. 2d 335 (D. Md. 1999).
12. Ibid., 336.
13. Ibid., 338.
14. Ibid.

15. Ibid., 339, quoting Massie v. Henry, 455 F.2d 779, 783 (4th Cir. 1972).
16. Ibid.
17. Ibid. (internal citation and quotation marks omitted).
18. Ibid.
19. Ibid., 338.
20. Ibid.
21. 489 F. Supp. 2d 139 (N.D.N.Y. 2006).
22. Ibid., 142.
23. Ibid., 145.
24. Ibid., 146.
25. 316 F. Supp. 185 (D.N.H. 1970).
26. Ibid., 186.
27. Ibid., 187.
28. Ibid., 186.
29. Ibid., 188.
30. Ibid.
31. Ibid.
32. Ibid., 189.
33. Ibid., 188–89.
34. 401 F.3d 381 (6th Cir. 2005).
35. Ibid., 385–86.
36. Ibid., 386.
37. Ibid.
38. Boroff v. Van Wert City Board of Education, 220 F.3d 465 (6th Cir. 2000).
39. Blau v. Fort Thomas School District, 401 F.3d at 388.
40. Ibid.
41. Ibid., citing Spence v. Washington, 418 U.S. 405, 411 (1974) and Texas v. Johnson, 491 U.S. 397, 404 (1989).
42. Ibid., 390.
43. *See* Meyer v. Nebraska, 262 U.S. 390 (1923) (statute prohibiting the teaching of school subjects in any language other than English was an arbitrary interference with parents' right to control the education of their children); Pierce v. Society of Sisters, 268 U.S. 510 (1925) (statute requiring all children between the ages of 8 and 16 to attend a public school unreasonably interfered with parents' right to direct the upbringing of their children. For a discussion of the parental right to direct and the responsibility of the state to educate its citizens, see Todd A. DeMitchell & Joseph J. Onosko, "A Parent's Child and the State's Future Citizen: Judicial and Legislative Responses to the Tension Over the Right to Direct an Education," 22, *Southern California Interdisciplinary Law Journal* 591 (2013).
44. Blau v. Fort Thomas Public School District, 401 F.3d at 395 (emphasis by the court).
45. Ibid., 395–96.
46. No. 1:07-cv-00936-JDT-WTL, 2007 U.S. Dist. LEXIS 57428 (S.D. Ind. Aug. 6, 2007).
47. Ibid., 4 (LexisNexis pagination).
48. Ibid., 5.
49. Ibid.
50. Ibid., 22.
51. 290 Fed. Appx. 273, 276 (11th Cir. 2008).
52. Ibid., 274.
53. Ibid., 275.
54. Ibid., 277.
55. Smith v. Goguen, 415 U.S. 566, 573 (1974).
56. Connally v. General Construction Company, 269 U.S. 385, 391 (1926).
57. Broadrick v. Oklahoma, 413 U.S. 601, 615 (1973).

58. Chalifoux v. New Caney Independent School District, 976 F. Supp. 659, 664 (S.D. Tex. 1997). The policy stated:

"1. Oversized apparel, including baggy pants which are worn low on the waist; overalls with one strap unfastened; pants that are cut off below the knees and worn with knee socks. (Pants should fit at the waist and have properly sewn hems).

2. Any attire which identifies students as a group (gang-related) may not be worn to school or school-related activities.

3. Baseball caps, hair nets, bandanas, sweatbands."

59. Ibid., 667.

60. Ibid., 669.

61. Stephenson v. Davenport Community School District, 110 F.3d 1303 (8th Cir. 1997).

62. Ibid., 1310 (internal quotations and citation omitted).

63. Ibid., 1311.

64. The court wrote, "Thus, the essentially unfettered discretion of these individuals placed a high school student in the unenviable position of removing her tattoo by scarring her body or suffering suspension from her educational pursuits for ten days and face possible expulsion. The District regulation, therefore, violates a central purpose of the vagueness doctrine that if arbitrary and discriminatory enforcement is to be prevented, laws must provide explicit standards for those who apply them." Ibid.

65. 827 F. Supp. 1459, 1460 (C.D. Calif. 1993).

66. Ibid.

67. Ibid., 1461.

68. Ibid., 1462.

69. Stephenson v. Davenport Community School District, 110 F.3d at 1311.

70. Blau v. Fort Thomas Public School District, 401 F.3d at 390.

71. Tinker v. Des Moines Independent Community School District, 393 U.S. 503, 507–8 (1969).

FOUR

Drugs, Politics, and the Confederate Battle Flag

Targeted Messages on Students' Clothing

Public symbolism has profound implications for the citizens of the public body represented by the symbol.

—Robert J. Bein[1]

When the United States Supreme Court decided the *Tinker* case in 1969, it may not have realized that it had opened the floodgates to a new type of lawsuit against school districts—what we might call "T-shirt litigation." In the years following the *Tinker* decision, students and their parents filed numerous lawsuits challenging the authority of school authorities to ban messages on students' clothing. The Tinker children's expression had consisted of a political statement—opposition to the war in Vietnam, which they communicated by wearing black armbands. But in the years following the Supreme Court's *Tinker* decision, the federal courts have reviewed numerous disputes between students and school administrators involving clothing-based student speech on a wide range of issues: politics, drugs, and even the Confederate battle flag.

As it happened, the *Tinker* case was decided about the time the T-shirt was evolving from a utilitarian men's undergarment to a fashionable item of clothing for both men and women. Moreover, beginning in the 1960s, people increasingly began wearing T-shirts with messages; and these messages ranged from profound political and social statements to humorous gag lines and bawdy expressions of sexual humor.[2] Indeed, when one reviews more than forty years of First Amendment lawsuits brought by students against school districts, a great many of them revolve around controversial and arguably inappropriate messages on students' T-shirts.

Although each of these legal disputes involves unique facts and unique student messages, most of them can be divided into three categories: 1) political and social topics, 2) drugs and alcohol, and 3) the Confederate battle flag. These categories of student-clothing disputes will be discussed separately in this chapter.

POLITICAL MESSAGES AND MESSAGES ON SOCIAL ISSUES

The Supreme Court's *Tinker* decision involved pure political speech — opposition to the Vietnam War, which students expressed symbolically by wearing black armbands at school. When the Supreme Court issued its opinion in the case, it seemed likely the justices anticipated that future conflicts between students and schools over students' free speech rights would involve serious political and social issues.

Thus, when reviewing student speech expressed on students' clothing, it is appropriate to begin with clothing messages on social and political topics. As we will see, when federal courts have evaluated these cases, they have usually looked to *Tinker* for guidance and asked whether the students' speech created a substantial disruption in the school environment.

> At least in high school, a political message does not justify a vulgar medium.
>
> *Pyle v. South Hadley School Committee*, 861, F. Supp. 157, 169 (D.Mass. 1994).

For example, in *Barber v. Dearborn Public Schools*, Breton Barber, a student at Dearborn High School in Dearborn, Michigan, wore a T-shirt to school that displayed a photograph of President George W. Bush along with the phrase, "International Terrorist."[3] Breton's school had a sizable Arab population; the school principal, Judith Coebly, feared Barber's message would offend these students, who by and large supported President Bush's policies in the Middle East. These events took place as the United States prepared to invade Iraq in 2001, and Principal Coebly also feared Breton's shirt would exacerbate tensions at the school, where some students had ties to military families. Thus, she prohibited Breton from wearing the T-shirt to school.

Breton sued the Dearborn school district and asked the court for an injunction requiring school authorities to allow him to wear his "International Terrorist" T-shirt at school. In response, Dearborn school authorities argued that they reasonably believed Breton's T-shirt would create a substantial disruption at his high school when they banned the shirt and thus it could be constitutionally banned under the *Tinker* standard.

A federal court was not persuaded, however, and granted Breton Barber his injunction. The court pointed out that there was no evidence of any disturbance or disruption at the high school on the day Breton wore his controversial T-shirt. The school defendants maintained that the T-shirt controversy had created a "media frenzy," which provided an additional justification for banning the shirt; but an assistant principal admitted "that there [had] not been any kind of demonstration, disruption, or commotion as a result of the media's presence."[4]

Finally, the court rejected Principal Coebly's argument that the imminent prospect of war between the United States and Iraq had created tensions that justified the ban. "Clearly the tension between students who support and those who oppose President Bush's decision to invade Iraq is no greater than the tension that existed during the United States' involvement in Vietnam between supporters of the war and war protesters," the court observed.[5]

Similarly, the Second Circuit Court of Appeals ruled that a T-shirt depicting President George W. Bush with the description "Chicken Hawk in Chief" and linking him to alcohol and drugs was in poor taste but was constitutionally protected.[6] Zachary Guiles was a seventh grade student when he first wore the T-shirt to school that displayed a disrespectful image of President George W. Bush.

This is how the court described Zachary's T-shirt:

> The front of the shirt, at the top, has large print that reads "George W. Bush," below it is the text, "Chicken-Hawk-In-Chief." Directly below these words is a large picture of the President's face, wearing a helmet, superimposed on the body of a chicken. Surrounding the President are images of oil rigs and dollar symbols. To one side of the President, three lines of cocaine and a razor blade appear. In the "chicken wing" of the President nearest the cocaine, there is a straw. In the other "wing" the President is holding a martini glass with an olive in it. Directly below all these depictions is printed, "1st Chicken Hawk Wing," and below that is text reading "World Domination Tour."[7]

The back of the T-shirt displayed similar images but also included smaller print accusing the president of being a crook, a cocaine addict, a draft dodger, and a drunk driver.[8] At least one student complained about the T-shirt. When Guiles was asked to tape over the offending images, turn the shirt inside out, or change it, he refused and was suspended.

Guiles brought suit seeking to enjoin the school from enforcing the dress code with regard to his T-shirt.[9] The federal district court found the images offensive or inappropriate under *Fraser* and declined to issue Guiles an injunction. However, the court also held that the school violated Guiles's free speech when it censored the word "cocaine." The dress code survived but the suspension did not, and the court ordered the school district to expunge all records of Guiles's suspension. Both parties appealed.

The Second Circuit Court of Appeals first reviewed the applicability of *Tinker, Fraser,* and *Hazelwood.* The court ruled that *Hazelwood* was inapplicable to the case because Guiles's T-shirt was not school sponsored. However, the Second Circuit concluded that the district court had mistakenly applied *Fraser* to Guiles's T-shirt.

The shirt did not contain vulgar, obscene, or profane language, the court asserted. Nor did the shirt's messages rise to a level of offensiveness that would allow Guiles's shirt to be banned under *Bethel.*[10] The court conceded that the alcohol and cocaine pictures on the shirt might cause displeasure and could be considered insulting and in poor taste, but they were not plainly offensive under the *Bethel* standard, "especially when considering that they are part of an anti-drug political message."[11]

Having dismissed the applicability of *Hazelwood* and *Fraser,* the Second Circuit then considered whether the school district could constitutionally ban Guiles's T-shirt under *Tinker's* disruptiveness standard. The appellate court concluded that the shirt had caused no disruption at Guiles's school and was unlikely to cause a disruption in the future. The Second Circuit Court of Appeals granted the injunction permitting him to wear his T-shirt and the record of his suspension was expunged. It is important to note that the dress code was not found unconstitutional; only its application to Guiles's T-shirt was affected.

Guiles involved political speech on national issues, but a Seventh Circuit decision involved politics at the school level. In 2007, the Seventh Circuit Court of Appeals heard a class action suit on behalf of twenty-four so-called gifted eighth graders (the "gifties") who were disciplined for wearing a T-shirt that lost a contest for the design of the class T-shirt. The T-shirts were worn as a protest against the way the T-shirt election was held. The plaintiffs found little sympathy for their cause with the Court of Appeals.

The students wore their T-shirts to school on the day that mandatory tests were being held, figuring that "the school would not take disciplinary action against them on that day, lest that lower the school's average test score (they were gifties after all)."[12] The court asserted that the students had avenues available in which to protest the T-shirt election that were "potentially less disruptive" than wearing the T-shirts in contravention of the principal's orders. In the end, the court held that the students had no protected-speech right to wear clothing of their own design; "clothing as such is not—normally at any rate—constitutionally protected."[13]

The Politics of Divisiveness

In *Sypniewski v. Warren Hills Regional Board of Education*, the Tenth Circuit Court of Appeals issued a lengthy and somewhat complicated decision that addressed whether school officials in New Jersey's Warren Hills Regional School District could constitutionally bar Thomas Sypniewski, a high school student, from wearing a T-shirt to school that was emblazoned with Jeff Foxworthy "redneck" jokes.[14] Thomas wore the shirt to school for most of a school day without incident, but he was suspended during the last period after he refused a request by the school's vice principal to turn the shirt inside out.

School authorities claimed that the "redneck" shirt violated the school's dress code, which barred clothing that displayed references to alcohol or sexual innuendo. They also maintained that the "redneck" reference violated the school district's racial harassment policy and might incite racial violence in a school that had had a history of racial tensions.

As the court explained, the school district had adopted its racial harassment policy after experiencing considerable racial tensions involving display of the Confederate flag on campus and the activities of a student gang known as the "Hicks." School authorities believed the term "redneck' was an identifier for the Hicks, and thus "redneck" was a gang identifier.[15]

Thomas Sypniewski and his two brothers (also students in the school district) sued, seeking an injunction against enforcement of the school's dress code and racial harassment policy. A federal trial judge upheld the constitutionality of the racial harassment policy, and the brothers appealed the ruling to the Tenth Circuit.

On appeal, the Tenth Circuit reversed the trial court, ruling that the Sypniewski brothers were entitled to a preliminary injunction prohibiting the school district from applying its racial harassment policy to prohibit the wearing of the "redneck" T-shirt. In the appellate court's view, there was "little or no evidence that the word 'redneck' had been used to harass or intimidate, or otherwise to offend."[16] Moreover, the court concluded, evidence revealed "a history of unproblematic use of the word, and that it was not associated to a significant degree with the Hicks or their behavior."[17]

Although the Tenth Circuit commended the Warren Hills school authorities for making a good faith effort to deal with racial tensions, "the application of the [racial harassment] policy to the Foxworthy T-shirt appears to go too far." School officials simply had not established that the shirt might threaten to disrupt the school or that it had violated any particular provision of its racial harassment policy.

A later court opinion involving a gang of rednecks turned out better for the school district. In *Governor Wentworth Regional School District v. Hendrickson*, Paul Hendrickson, a high school student identified as a member of a "gay group," came to school wearing a so-called No Nazis patch, which consisted of a swastika on which was superimposed the international "no" symbol—"a red circle with a diagonal line through it."[18] Although the patch was characterized in various ways, Hendrickson himself called it a "'tolerance patch' signifying values of tolerance and acceptance."[19]

As the court explained in great detail, Hendrickson's gay group was in an ongoing conflict with a rival group known as the "homophobes" or the "rednecks." School officials had documented several incidents of bullying and threats of violence, and the rednecks sometimes taunted members of the gay group with the Nazi salute, "Seig Heil."[20]

In light of the serious tensions between the gay group and the homophobes, school authorities worried that Hendrickson's "No Nazis" patch might spark a school disruption and even lead to violence. Out of safety concerns, they directed him not to wear his patch to school.

Hendrickson repeatedly refused to comply. At first, he was sent home for the day when he appeared at school wearing the "No Nazi" patch. Eventually, he was suspended with the proviso that he could not return to school wearing the patch. According to the court, Hendrickson was out of school for several days or even weeks.

Eventually, the school district took the extraordinary step of filing a declaratory action in federal court, seeking a judicial ruling that it had the authority to prohibit Hendrickson from wearing the "No Nazi" patch at school. The Governor Wentworth Regional School District then filed for summary judgment, asking the judge to affirm the constitutionality of its conduct.

After an exhaustive analysis, the court sided with the school district, ruling that it had lawfully banned Hendrickson's patch, based on reasonable concerns about the patch's potential for a serious disruption at school. As the court put it,

> It was reasonable for school authorities to conclude, under all the circumstances that if Hendrickson were permitted to wear the patch, it would likely precipitate further discord, tension, harassment, and disruptive, even potentially violent, behavior at school. That in turn would disrupt the educational environment and jeopardize the safety of not only the members of the "gay" and "redneck" groups, but all students, teachers, and staff as well.[21]

Madrid v. Anthony is another federal court decision with themes of tensions between rival groups of students.[22] In that case, students and parents sued the Cypress-Fairbanks Independent School District and David Anthony, the school superintendent, after a high school principal banned students from wearing T-shirts that said, "We Are Not Criminals" and "Border Patrol."

The controversy took place in the context of a school walkout at Cypress Ridge High School that was staged by Hispanic students who opposed proposed immigration legislation pending in Congress, which they considered unfair and punitive. Some students, mostly Hispanic, wore T-shirts to school on the day of the walkout that read "We Are Not Criminals." This walkout occurred on a Monday.

Claudio Garcia, the high school principal, did not punish the students for the Monday walkout, but he warned them they would be punished if they walked out again. Based on the rumor that white and African American students who opposed the walkout were going to antagonize Hispanic students by wearing T-shirts to school that said "Border Patrol," Principal Garcia feared a race riot would erupt. Consequently, he banned students from wearing either "Border Patrol" T-shirts or "We Are Not Criminals" T-Shirts.

Disregarding Principal Garcia's warning, about 130 students walked out of school on Tuesday. These students were suspended, and on Wednesday, school authorities contacted the suspended students' parents and asked them pick up their children at school.

When the parents arrived at the school, some of them demanded to speak with Principal Garcia. Finding the group too large to meet with in one gathering, Garcia asked parents to make appointments. Some of the parents milled around the school building, and eventually a security officer asked them to leave the premises.

In due course, some parents and students who were involved in these events sued the school district, alleging that the ban on the "We Are Not Criminals" T-shirt violated students' right to free speech and that the request for parents to leave the school building violated their constitutional right to assembly. They also charged school officials with refusing to allow Hispanic students to go to the restroom on the day following the walkout in retaliation for their participation in the immigration protests.

In essence, the Cypress-Fairbanks school authorities admitted they that had prohibited students from wearing T-shirts that expressed their opinions, that they asked parents to leave the school premises, and that they had prohibited students from leaving class on the day after the first walkout, which prevented some of them from using the restroom. Officials argued, however, that they prohibited the T-shirts and barred students from going to the restroom during class on one tense school day in order to prevent riots. Moreover, they explained, school authorities asked parents to leave the school premises on the day of the student suspensions because they could not meet with so many parents at once and they were statutorily required to protect each student's privacy.

A federal trial judge found the school district's arguments persuasive and granted their motion for summary judgment. Regarding the T-shirt ban, the court ruled that school officials have the authority to prevent problems before they happen; they are not required to wait until a disturbance occurs before taking action. In the case before it, the court noted that students had already disrupted the work of the school when they walked out of school on Monday. "The evidence shows school officials held a reasonable belief that wearing the t-shirts at issue would cause further, perhaps even more severe disruption and put student safety at risk," the court wrote.[23]

Thus, in the court's opinion, Principal Garcia's decision to ban the T-shirts was constitutionally permissible under *Tinker*'s substantial disruption standard:

> [F]aced with hundreds of students who were disrupting the educational process and two-thirds of the student body who might have antagonized the Hispanic students by wearing a Border Patrol t-shirt, the Court finds Principal Garcia made the proper decision to ban the t-shirts in order to *protect* the Hispanic students from the animosity of other students, not to harm them by precluding their speech. Based on these facts, the Court reasonably believed it necessary to prohibit students from wearing both t-shirts at issue because the expression on them would exacerbate hostility within the student body and could cause fights that would materially and substantially interfere with the work of the school.[24]

The court also found that school officials acted reasonably when they requested parents to leave the Cypress Ridge High School premises and that their decision to prohibit students from leaving class on the day following the first walkout was also reasonable. Neither action, the court concluded, was motivated by a desire to violate constitutional rights or retaliate against the plaintiffs.

Dariano v. Morgan Hill Unified School District Live Oak High School is another student free speech case set in the context of school tensions over immigration and ethnic tensions.[25] In this case, three students at a California high school brought suit alleging a violation of their rights to free expression when they were not allowed to wear American flag shirts on Cinco de Mayo Day.[26] The assistant principal asked the students to turn their shirts inside out based on his belief that the shirts could reasonably result in disruption.

The federal district court began its analysis by recognizing that courts have struggled to find the right balance between students' First Amendment rights and the need for the school administrators to maintain a safe educational environment. The court applied the *Tinker* two-prong analysis to the facts. Finding no disruption, no classes delayed, no classes interrupted, and no violence reported on the day that Assistant Principal Rodriquez asked the students to change their shirts, the court considered whether school officials might reasonably have forecast a substantial disruption if the students had been allowed to wear their flag-themed shirts.

The facts showed that for the previous six years there had been thirty fights on campus. Some of the fights involved gangs, and other fights were between Caucasian and Hispanic students. On the previous Cinco de Mayo, a verbal exchange and altercation between Hispanic and white students erupted over a makeshift American flag placed on one of the trees on campus in response to Mexican students walking around school with the Mexican flag. On the day the plaintiff students wore the American flag shirts, a female student approached one of the plaintiffs, motioned to the shirt and said, "[W]hy are you wearing that, do you not like Mexicans?"[27] In addition, several students warned the school administration about potential disruption over the shirts.

Acknowledging that no actual violence or disruption occurred from wearing the American flag shirts, the court noted that the *Tinker* disruption is not an "actual disruption" standard. Rather, the school administrators need only articulate reasonable grounds, more than an inchoate sense of pending disruption, based on an established fact pattern. The schools need not ignore warnings and wait until violence occurs to take action. Principals and assistant principals cannot predict with certainty "which threats are empty and which will lead to true violence."[28]

In this case, the school officials acted reasonably in forecasting that violence could result from wearing the shirts. The assistant principal had asked students to wear their shirts inside out or remove them to avoid physical harm, not to abridge the students' free speech rights. Students who refused and were sent home received an excused absence. The restriction on wearing the shirts at that time was upheld.

The Ninth Circuit Court of Appeals unanimously affirmed the district court's use of *Tinker* to establish that the administration had forecast a substantial disruption based on previous incidents of threats, ongoing racial tension, gang violence, and a near-violent altercation over the display of the American flag at the last Cinco de Mayo celebration. School officials do not need to wait until actual disruption occurs to take action. Citing one of their 1973 cases, they added context to the reasonable forecast requirement, writing, "'the level of disturbance required to justify official intervention is relatively lower in a public school than it might be on a street corner.'"[29]

We conclude this section on divisive student speech, this time focusing on potential religious divisiveness, with a review of *Boroff v. Van Wert City Board of Education,* in which the Sixth Circuit Court of Appeals upheld a school ban on so-called Marilyn Manson T-shirts, not under the *Tinker* standard, which would have permitted the shirts to be banned if they created a substantial disruption in the school environment, but under the *Fraser* standard.[30] The Sixth Circuit said simply that the T-shirts conveyed a message that was contrary to the educational mission of the school; and thus, under *Fraser,* they could be banned.

These are the facts of the *Boroff* case. Nicholas Boroff, a senior at Van Wert High School in Ohio, came to school wearing a "Marilyn Manson" T-shirt, which the Sixth Circuit court described as follows: "The front of the T-shirt depicted a three-faced Jesus, accompanied by the words "See No Truth. Hear No Truth. Speak No Truth." On the back of the shirt, the word "BELIEVE" was spelled out in capital letters, with the letters "LIE" highlighted. Marilyn Manson's name (although not his picture) was displayed prominently on the front of the shirt."[31]

Marilyn Manson, as the Sixth Circuit opinion explained, was the stage name for "goth" rock singer Brian Warner, and also the name of the band in which he was the lead singer. According to the court, Manson (the individual) was widely regarded as a user of illegal drugs, which he had not denied. Indeed, one of his songs was titled "I Don't Like the Drugs (But the Drugs Like Me)."[32]

At the time of these events, Nicholas's high school had a "Dress and Grooming" policy, which stated "clothing with offensive illustrations, drug, alcohol, or tobacco slogans . . . are not acceptable."[33] One of the school principal's aides spotted Nicholas wearing the shirt and told him it was offensive. The aide gave Nicholas three choices: He could turn the shirt inside out, he could go home to get a different shirt, or he could leave the school and be considered truant. Nicholas left school.

The following day, Nicholas wore another Marilyn Manson T-shirt to school. That same day, Nicholas and his mother met with the school superintendent, the high school principal, and the principal's aide. The superintendent told mother and son that students would not be permitted to wear Marilyn Manson T-shirts to school.

In defiance of this directive, Nicholas wore different Marilyn Manson T-shirts to school on each of the next three school days. These shirts displayed pictures of Marilyn Manson, whose appearance, the Sixth Court noted, could "fairly be described as ghoulish and creepy."[34] Each day, school authorities told Nicholas he was not permitted to wear a Marilyn Manson shirt to school.

Less than a month after this dispute erupted, Nicholas's mother filed suit, claiming that school administrators had violated her son's First Amendment right to free expression by refusing to allow him to wear Marilyn Manson T-shirts to school. A federal district court dismissed the suit, and she appealed. At some point in the litigation, Nicholas turned eighteen, and his name was substituted for that of his mother's in the lawsuit.

On appeal, Nicholas argued that the school's ban on Marilyn Manson T-shirts was unreasonable and pointed out that school officials allowed students to wear T-shirts promoting other bands. He also maintained that there was no evidence that a substantial disruption would arise if he wore a Marilyn Manson T-shirt to school.

The Sixth Circuit rejected these arguments and upheld the trial court's dismissal of his suit. "The standard for reviewing the suppression of vulgar or plainly offensive speech is governed by *Fraser*," the court noted.[35] "The School in this case . . . found the Marilyn Manson T-shirts to be offensive because the band promotes destructive conduct and demoralizing values that are contrary to the educational mission of the school."[36]

Specifically, the court noted that the high school principal "found the 'three-headed Jesus' T-shirt to be offensive because of the 'See No Truth. Hear No Truth. Speak No Truth.' mantra on the front, and because of the obvious implication of the word 'BELIEVE' with 'LIE' highlighted on the back."[37] In the principal's view, which the Sixth Circuit quoted approvingly, "'the distorted Jesus figure was offensive, because 'mocking any religious figure is contrary to our educational mission which is to be respectful of others and others' beliefs.'"[38]

One Sixth Circuit judge dissented from the majority's opinion, arguing that the school had engaged in viewpoint discrimination by banning Nicholas's T-shirt because of the viewpoint it expressed on religion. The majority strenuously objected to this interpretation of the evidence. In the majority's opinion," the record demonstrates that the School prohibited Boroff's Marilyn Manson T-shirts generally because this particular rock group promotes disruptive and demoralizing values which are inconsistent with and counter-productive to education."[39]

Firearms: Free Speech and the Right to "Depict" Arms

Using the reasoning of *Morse* as applied to drugs, schools have the authority to restrict clothing that promotes and glorifies violence. However, schools go overboard when they restrict clothing that only depicts benign depictions of weapons. Dress codes that respond to any depiction of a firearm or weapons have resulted in legal challenges.

For example, in *Griggs v. Fort Wayne School Board*, David Arnold Griggs, an Elmhurst High School student, came to school wearing a T-shirt depicting a portion of the Marine Corps Creed ("My Rifle") and a picture of an M16 rifle and the seal of the Marine Corps.[40] There were no complaints from students, nor was there any disruption as a result of his wearing the T-shirt. Nevertheless, the school authorities told Griggs he could not wear the T-shirt to school, citing the dress code that prohibited wearing any clothing that depicted symbols of violence. At the time Griggs wore his T-shirt to school, the community had recently been rocked by the kidnapping, brutal torture, and murder of Cherie Sue Hartman, a student at the same high school.[41]

Griggs brought suit in federal district court for a violation of his free speech rights under the First Amendment. The court held that the prohibition against "symbols of violence" was not overbroad and was reasonably related to a legitimate pedagogical concern of preventing violence at school.[42] However, "a permissible regulation might occasionally be used to censor more speech than the First Amendment allows."[43]

The court held that while preventing violence by prohibiting symbols of violence at school is permissible, the application of this dress-code section to Griggs's Marine Corps T-shirt went "a bit too far." It was not related to the tragic murder of Cherie Sue Hartman or the massacre at Columbine High School (arguments asserted by the school board),[44] and it did not disrupt the school.[45] The policy was constitutional but its application to the Griggs's T-shirt was not. There was no rational relationship between stopping violence in the school and the message on Griggs's T-shirt that Marines must fight America's enemies.

Next we turn to a couple of cases involving students who appeared at school wearing T-shirts that displayed firearms. In *Newsome v. Albemarle County School Board*, a 2003 decision, the Fourth Circuit Court of Appeals upheld the right of Alan Newsome, a Virginia sixth grader, to wear a T-shirt to school that depicted figures pointing weapons, finding the school district's policy against student messages that related to weapons was unconstitutionally overbroad.[46] As described by the court, the back of Alan's T-shirt, which was purple in color, depicted "three black silhouettes of men holding firearms superimposed on the letters 'NRA' positioned above the phrase "SHOOTING SPORTS CAMP."[47] The front of his shirt "bore a smaller but identical version of the men superimposed on the initials 'NRA,' but no other writing or symbols."[48]

Elizabeth Pitt, assistant principal at Alan's school, saw the T-shirt and had the immediate impression that the silhouette figures were "sharp-shooters," which reminded her of the Columbine High School shootings. In her judgment, the images on Alan's T-shirt could "reasonably be interpreted by other middle-school students to promote the use of guns." In addition, she concluded "that the imagery on the t-shirt was at odds with her obligation as a school administrator to discourage and prevent gun-related violence since the images on Newsome's t-shirt conflicted with the message that 'Guns and Schools Don't Mix' and had the potential to create confusion among middle school students over the appropriate boundaries between firearms and schools."[49]

Assistant Principal Pitt persuaded Alan to turn the shirt inside out. Later the school district amended its student/parent handbook to prohibit students from wearing "messages on clothing, jewelry, and personal belongings that relate to drugs, alcohol, tobacco, weapons, violence, sex, vulgarity, or that reflect adversely upon persons because of their race or ethnic group."[50]

A few months later, Alan sued the Albemarle County School Board, alleging that his First Amendment rights had been violated when he was directed to turn his shirt inside out and that the school district's dress code was unconstitutionally overbroad and vague. A trial court denied Alan's request for a preliminary injunction, and Alan appealed.

On appeal, the Fourth Circuit reversed the trial court, finding that the school board's dress code, which prohibited all student speech that "related" to weapons, was unconstitutionally overbroad. The court pointed out that the school district had presented no evidence before the trial court that any student clothing containing a message relating to weapons had ever caused a substantial disruption in the school environment.

Moreover, the dress code prohibited the display of "lawful, nonviolent, and nonthreatening symbols of not only popular, but important organizations and ideals."[51] By way of example, the court pointed out that the State Seal of the Commonwealth of Virginia depicted a woman, "standing with one foot on the chest of a vanquished tyrant, holding a spear."[52] The court also noted the irony of the fact that the school district's own high school mascot was a patriot armed with a musket.

The *Newsome* case certainly highlights the importance of a tightly drafted dress code. Had the policy explicitly prohibited student speech that promotes violence instead of speech that "related" to weapons, perhaps the school district would have prevailed.

This brings us to *Miller v. Penn Manor School District*, a federal district court opinion with facts somewhat similar to the *Newsome* case.[53] In this case, Donald Miller, a high school student, wore a T-shirt to school, which the court described as follows:

> The T-shirt prominently displays images of an automatic handgun on the front pocket area and back of the T-shirt. The front pocket of the T-shirt is also imprinted with the statement "Volunteer Homeland Security" with the image of an automatic handgun placed between the word "Volunteer" above the handgun and the words "Homeland Security" below the handgun.
>
> The back of the T-shirt is imprinted with the statement "Special Issue-Resident-Lifetime License, United States Terrorist Hunting Permit, Permit No. 91101, Gun Owner-No Bag Limit" in block letters superimposed over a larger automatic weapon.[54]

As the court explained, Donald obtained the shirt as a gift from his uncle, a member of the U.S. military, who had purchased it from the Fort Benning Post Exchange. At the time of the litigation, Donald's uncle was stationed in Iraq.

Although the case includes a detailed discussion about the Penn Manor School District's dress code and its revisions, the heart of the dispute between Donald and the school district hinged on the fact that school authorities banned Donald's T-shirt because they believed it promoted violence and was unacceptable clothing in the school environment. The district's dress code, as revised, prohibited "messages that advocate violence and mayhem, criminal behavior or the violation of Board policy."[55]

Before the court, Donald argued that his T-shirt's message represented "political and patriotic speech aimed at supporting our troops fighting the war on terror in Afghanistan and Iraq" and was also an expression of support for his uncle, who was fighting in Iraq. The school district countered that it was entitled to ban Donald's T-shirt without a showing of substantial disruption under *Tinker* because it had the constitutional authority "to prohibit student speech that advocates the use of force, violence and violation of law."[56]

In support of its argument, the school district cited *Morse v. Frederick*,[57] in which the Supreme Court upheld a school principal's ban on a student banner that the principal believed contained a message promoting the use of illegal drugs. In that case, the Supreme Court said that schools have an important interest in discouraging illegal drug use among students, and thus they need not tolerate student speech that promotes such use. By extension, the school defendants argued, the school district had a vital interest in curbing violence in the schools and could bar student speech that advocates violence without offending the First Amendment.

Although the trial court invalidated part of the school district's policies on constitutional grounds, it upheld the district's decision to ban Donald's T-shirt based on the shirt's message, which endorsed the use of violence. "The language of Donald's T-shirt advocates the use of force, violence, and violation of law in the form of illegal vigilante behavior and the hunting and killing of human beings," the court observed. "Accordingly," the court ruled, "based on the Supreme Court's post-*Tinker* jurisprudence, I conclude that defendants do not have to demonstrate substantial disruption to restrict Donald from wearing his T-shirt."[58]

Miller v. Penn Manor School District is a significant decision because a federal court upheld a school district's student-speech ban without relying on the *Tinker* substantial disruption standard. Although the court did not make clear which judicial precedents it relied upon, it apparently concluded that a school district's interest in preventing violence in schools, like its interest in discouraging student drug use, gave Penn Manor the constitutional authority to ban Donald Miller's T-shirt without the necessity of showing that the shirt was disruptive, or likely to be disruptive, in the school environment. Thus, the court implicitly used the Supreme Court's 2007 *Morse v. Frederick* opinion as the judicial guidance for its decision.

The *Miller* case, like the *Boroff* case, upheld a school ban on student expression without relying on *Tinker*'s substantial disruption test. Both cases illustrate efforts by federal judges to find an alternative legal justification for banning student clothing-based messages when the messages do not appear likely to create a school disruption. Certain messages, some courts are now saying, can be banned because they run counter to the mission of the schools, which includes the authority to promote civility and discourage violence.

CLOTHING MESSAGES ABOUT DRUGS AND ALCOHOL

Just as high school students often exhibit a strong interest in sex, many are fascinated with illegal drugs and alcohol. One might think, therefore, that there would be a lot of cases involving students who claim a constitutional right to express their views about drugs and alcohol on T-shirts or other items of clothing.

In fact, there are very few lawsuits in which students have claimed a First Amendment right to proclaim their support of alcohol use or the illegal use of drugs. Perhaps potential plaintiffs realize that such a lawsuit would probably not be favorably received in a federal court.

For example, as the Fourth Circuit noted in a 1980 case involving a school's suppression of an underground student publication that contained an advertisement for drug paraphernalia, an advertisement promoting the use of drugs "encourages action which . . . endanger the health and safety of students."[59] The court ruled that the school principal had the authority to halt distribution of any materials of that nature without regard to whether the publication was likely to create a substantial disruption of school activities.

Relying primarily on *Fraser*, an Idaho federal district court denied a student's motion for a preliminary injunction that would allow him to wear a T-shirt to school that depicted school administrators imbibing alcoholic beverages. The student's T-shirt portrayed a caricature of three of the school administrators (the principal, a vice principal, and a dean) drinking alcohol and acting drunk on school property.[60] The drawing showed each administrator with a different alcoholic beverage and a case of beer sitting nearby. The caption read, "It doesn't get any better than this," referring to a then current beer commercial.[61]

Apparently, the student planned to sell T-shirts with this caricature during homecoming week. When the plan was discovered, school officials suspended the student for two days. When the student returned to school, he wore the controversial T-shirt and was sent home and told to change his shirt. A federal court upheld the school's decision to take disciplinary action and rejected the student's argument that his free speech rights were violated.

In a case that foreshadowed *Morse*, the Fourth Circuit ruled that a school need not tolerate student speech that runs counter to the school's educational position on a prohibited substance. The court stated that schools in Idaho are statutorily directed to teach students about the effects of alcohol. The court cited *Fraser* for the proposition that teaching can only occur within a "civilized context," and that teaching occurs when the school, through its educators, "sets the bounds for proper conduct."[62]

The federal district court pointed out that the T-shirt caricature conveyed the false impression that school administrators consume alcohol on school grounds, which is a misdemeanor offense. This false depiction compromised the role model that administrators are required to uphold, which causes harm to the administrators. Moreover, the plaintiff suffered little to no harm from the school's prohibition against wearing the T-shirt. Therefore, his request for a preliminary injunction was not warranted.

Students who argue they have the First Amendment right to promote the use of drugs and alcohol on their clothing have a poor track record in the federal courts. Courts have no difficulty rejecting these claims under *Morse*, which clearly held that schools need not tolerate student speech that celebrates the illegal use of drugs. Moreover, at least one federal court looked to *Fraser* to make the point that schools may ban student clothing that falsely conveys the message that school administrators imbibe alcoholic beverages at a school activity.

THE CONFEDERATE BATTLE FLAG

The last category of clothing-based student expression that we will examine in this chapter is student clothing that displays a Confederate flag—usually the iconic Confederate battle flag. "Without question, Confederate flags are controversial."[63] Again and again, the federal courts have been called to determine whether students have a First Amendment right to display a Confederate flag on their clothing while at school. A surprisingly large number of these cases have reached the federal appellate court level, which is an indication of how strongly some students and parents feel about the right to display a Confederate flag.

Confederate flag litigation in the federal courts dates back to the early 1970s, and it is not necessary to examine all of these cases in detail to understand the present state of the law on the constitutionality of school prohibitions against students wearing Confederate flags on their clothing while at school.[64] In this section we will examine some of the recent federal appellate court decisions on this issue.

As we will see, schools win most of these cases. In general, the courts have applied *Tinker*'s substantial-disruption test to the facts of these cases and have supported school authorities' decision to ban the Confederate flag if they have evidence that displaying the flag will likely trigger a substantial disruption in the school environment, such as racial turmoil.

THE CONFEDERATE FLAG: SYMBOL OF WHAT?

Undoubtedly, the Confederate battle flag does not represent the same thing to everyone. . . . There are citizens of all races who view the flag as a symbolic acknowledgment of pride in Southern heritage and the ideals of independence. Likewise, there are citizens of all races who perceive the flag as embodying principles of discrimination, segregation, white supremacy, and rebellion.

Sons of Confederate Veterans, Inc. v. Glendening, 954 F. Supp. 1099, 1103 (D. Md. 1997) (internal quotation marks and internal citation omitted).

West v. Derby Unified School District, decided in 2000, involved a student known as "T.W." who was suspended from school after he drew a Confederate flag during his math class; he did not display the flag on his clothing.[65] The school district had previously promulgated a rule against displaying the Confederate flag and other racially offensive symbols, an action it took in response to significant racial tensions at the high school. Racist graffiti had appeared on the high school campus, and one fight had erupted over a student wearing a Confederate flag headband. Moreover, racial tensions had been exacerbated by the off-campus activities of the Ku Klux Klan and Aryan Nation.[66]

T.W.'s parent sued, alleging several constitutional violations, but the Tenth Circuit Court of Appeals had no trouble affirming the trial court's dismissal of the case. In the court's view, school officials had not violated T.W.'s First Amendment rights, since they "had reasonably concluded that possession or display of the Confederate flag images . . . would likely lead to a material and substantial disruption of school discipline."[67] The school district had passed a ban on displays of the Confederate flag, the court ruled, not merely to avoid discomfort and unpleasantness, but to avoid the possibility of serious racial conflict in the schools. Indeed, the lower court had specifically found that the school district had a reasonable basis for concluding that the Confederate flag is a symbol that "is racially divisive or creates ill will or hatred."[68] Thus, in the court's opinion, school officials had not violated T.W.'s free speech rights when it sanctioned him for drawing a Confederate flag while at school.

In *Scott v. School Board of Alachua County,* a 2003 opinion, two high school students defied their school principal's unwritten ban on the display of Confederate flags and were suspended.[69] They sued, but a Florida federal court upheld the suspension. The students then appealed, raising several legal arguments, including the argument that there was insufficient evidence of substantial disruption to justify their suspension.

The Eleventh Circuit Court of Appeals affirmed the trial court's decision, adopting part of it verbatim. In essence, the Eleventh Circuit affirmed the principal's Confederate flag ban under two principles. First, school officials had produced enough evidence of racial tensions to justify the ban under the *Tinker* standard on the grounds that they feared a substantial disruption if the flag was displayed.

Second, relying on *Fraser*, the court noted that a school's essential mission includes the responsibility "to teach students of differing races, creeds and colors to engage each other in civil terms rather than in terms of debate highly offensive or highly threatening to others."[70] In the court's opinion, there was "no evidence that the school district [had] attempted to suppress civil debate on racial matters." Rather, "the district had concluded that the display of certain symbols that have become associated with racial prejudice are so likely to provoke feelings of hatred and ill will in others that they are inappropriate in the school context."[71]

The *Scott* decision, like the *Miller* decision and the *Boroff* decision discussed earlier in this chapter, is another federal court decision that reached beyond *Tinker*'s disruption standard to approve a school ban on student expression. Essentially, the court concluded that the Confederate flag, when displayed in the school environment, could be viewed as offensive and uncivil speech and could be banned under *Fraser*'s offensive speech standard without regard to whether the speech might cause a substantial disruption. The court focused on the content of the message (*Fraser*) and not the response to the message (*Tinker*).

In *Barr v. Lafon*, a Sixth Circuit opinion, students challenged a school district's rule prohibiting students from displaying the Confederate flag on their clothing while at school.[72] As explained by the high school principal at a school assembly, he would not allow students "to have Rebel flags or symbols of [the] Rebel flag on their clothing, or anything else that was a disruption to the school."[73] Students sued, arguing they had a First Amendment right to express their Southern heritage by displaying the Confederate flag on their clothing, but a federal trial court was unsympathetic and dismissed their case.

On appeal, the students argued that the school district had engaged in viewpoint discrimination, prohibiting some racially divisive symbols but not others. In particular, the students charged the school with prohibiting students from displaying the Confederate flag on their clothing but allowing African American students to wear clothes that displayed an image of Malcolm X.

The Sixth Circuit agreed with the students that if there was evidence that the school district had enforced its dress code against the Confederate flag but not against other racially divisive symbols, it would be compelled to reverse the trial court's decision in the school district's favor.[74]

But in fact, the court concluded, the students had produced no more than "a scintilla of evidence" that this was the case.

Moreover, in the Sixth Circuit's opinion, there was ample evidence that school officials reasonable foresaw substantial disruption if students came to school wearing clothing that depicted the Confederate flag. "This is not a case in which the school acted upon undifferentiated fear or apprehension of disturbance," the court emphasized.[75] Rather, "in a context of high racial tensions, race-related altercations, and threats of violence," school authorities reasonably feared the flag would disrupt the school's educational process.[76]

In *B.W.A. v. Farmington R-7 School District*,[77] a 2009 decision out of Missouri, the Eighth Circuit Court of Appeals upheld a school district's ban on student clothing depicting the Confederate flag. Three students, identified only by initials, sued the Farmington School District after they were sent home for wearing various items of clothing that displayed the Confederate flag, including a belt buckle that contained an image of the flag and the words "Dixie Classic."

As explained by the court, Farmington's school superintendent had banned students from displaying the Confederate flag on their clothing prior to the suspensions. He took this action due to several racially charged incidents that had taken place during the previous school year. "In the first incident, a white student urinated on a fourth-grade black student while allegedly saying 'that is what black people deserve.'"[78] In the second incident, white students showed up at a black student's residence and made racial comments. A fight ensued, and later people drove around the black student's home "screaming racial epithets and threatening to burn down the home."[79] In a third incident, Farmington varsity basketball players allegedly made racial slurs toward two black players on an opposing team during a basketball tournament, which led to an investigation by the U.S. Justice Department's Office for Civil Rights.

The students sued the school district, alleging a violation of their constitutional rights, but a federal district court granted the school district's motion to dismiss the suit. On appeal, the Eighth Circuit affirmed. Based on the prior incidents of racial conflict, the court concluded that Farmington school officials reasonably forecast that there would be substantial disruption if the Confederate flag was displayed at the high school.

Similarly, in *A.M. v. Board of Trustees of Burleson Independent School District*, the Fifth Circuit Court of Appeals backed a Texas school district that prohibited two high school students from carrying purses on campus that displayed the Confederate flag.[80] The students sued and sought an injunction against the school ban. A Texas federal court denied their motion for an injunction and dismissed their suit, finding sufficient evidence that school officials reasonably anticipated a disruption if the Confederate flag was displayed on campus.

On appeal, the Fifth Circuit summarized the school district's considerable evidence supporting their claim that the Confederate flag would likely provoke a substantial disruption if displayed on campus:

> There is ample, uncontroverted evidence that elements of the BHS student body have continually manifested racial hostility and tension. This tension has become evident in the various events described above, including racially hostile graffiti and vandalism, multiple disciplinary referrals involving racial epithets, and a physical confrontation between white BHS students and the African-American students of another high school. Some of these elements included the use of the Confederate flag, including the incidents in which a white HS student waved the flag in the direction of an opposing school's predominantly African-American volleyball team. As recently as spring 2006, Confederate flags were flown over the flagpole on Martin Luther King Jr. Day and a white student simulated the lynching of an African-American student.[81]

Even if those incidents "[did] not rise to the level of "substantial disruption" under *Tinker* (thus justifying the ban based on past actual disruption)," the court observed, "they serve as a factual basis for administrators' forecast that disruptions might occur if students were allowed to display racially charged symbols such as the Confederate flag."[82]

In sum, the court concluded that school officials reasonably anticipated that displays of the Confederate flag would create a substantial disruption at Burleson High School. Moreover, contrary to the students' contention, it was not necessary for school officials to show that display of the flag had caused a disruption in the past before imposing a ban on its display.

Finally, we have the Fourth Circuit's 2013 opinion in *Hardwick v. Heyward*, the latest federal appellate court decision to consider whether a high school student has a First Amendment right to display a Confederate flag on the student's clothing while at school.[83] In that case, the Fourth Circuit concluded that a South Carolina school district did not violate the free speech rights of Candice Hardwick when it prohibited her from wearing a number of shirts that depicted the Confederate flag over a period of three school years.

In 2003, Candice Hardwick was a middle school student in the Latta School District (LSD), a small school system in South Carolina. The town of Latta had a heritage of slavery and segregation, and its schools were not desegregated until the 1970–1971 school year.[84] At the time of the litigation, LSD's student enrollment was approximately 1,600, about equally divided between white and African American students.

Latta Middle School and Latta High School both had student dress codes. The middle school dress code stated that student dress would generally be considered appropriate so long as it did not "distract others, interfere with the instructional program, or otherwise cause disruption."[85] The policy then went on to describe clothing that would be deemed inappropriate: "clothing that displays profane language, drugs, tobacco, or alcohol advertisements, sexual innuendoes or anything else deemed to be offensive."[86]

LSD's high school dress code was similar to the middle school policy. The high school code provided that

> [S]tudents are to come to school in a neat and clean manner each day. Dress is casual, but some styles, which may be appropriate outside of school, are clearly inappropriate for schools. Students may not wear the following: . . . Shirts with obscene/derogatory sayings.[87]

During the 2002–2003 school year, Candice had the first of a series of confrontations with school officials over her clothing. In early 2003, the middle school principal directed Candice to remove her "Southern Chick" shirt, which displayed a Confederate flag.

During the following school year (2003–2004), school officials told Candice to remove a "Dixie Angels" shirt, a "Southern Girls" shirt, and a shirt honoring African American Confederate soldiers. All these shirts depicted a Confederate flag. Candice also wore a shirt displaying the American flag with the words "Old Glory," and "Flew over legalized slavery for 90 years."

In late February 2004, Candice came to school wearing a shirt that depicted Robert E. Lee and the Confederate flag. She was given an in-school suspension after she refused to change shirts. The following month, Candice came to school wearing a "Girls Rule," shirt that displayed a Confederate flag. She changed shirts on this occasion after school authorities directed her to do so.

At some point in this ongoing confrontation, Candice's parents wrote a letter to John Kirby, the LSD superintendent, informing him that they approved of Candice's clothing choices, which reflected Candice's heritage and religious beliefs. LSD's school board chairman, Harold Kornblut, responded to the letter, telling the parents that LSD was justified in banning Candice's Confederate-flag clothing based on a long history of racial tensions in the school district and the likelihood that other students might interpret the flag's meaning differently from the way Candice interpreted it.

In 2004, Candice began attending Latta High School, where the Confederate-flag controversy continued. In May 2005, the high school principal removed Candice from class for wearing a shirt that proclaimed "Daddy's Little Redneck," and—like several of Candice's previous shirts—displayed a Confederate flag.

Candice then produced four more "protest" shirts. The principal prohibited these shirts as well, although not all the protest shirts contained pictures of the Confederate flag. For example, one protest shirt stated, "Honorary Member of the FBI: Federal Bigot Institutions."[88]

Unable to get LSD to change its position on her choice of Confederate-flag themed clothing, Candice sued her middle school principal, her high school principal, and the school district's board of trustees, claiming a violation of her constitutional rights under the First and Fourteenth Amendments. A federal trial court dismissed most of Candice's claims on the defendants' motion for summary judgment, and Candice filed her first appeal.

In its initial ruling, the Fourth Circuit ruled that it did not have jurisdiction over Candice's case since the trial court had not ruled on all of Candice's claims. Specifically, the trial court had not ruled on the so-called protest shirts that Candice wore—some of which did not contain images of the Confederate flag. The trial court then ruled on the protest shirt issues, dismissing Candice's suit in its entirety; and Candice filed her second appeal.

In its second decision on Hardwick's case, the Fourth Circuit Court of Appeals affirmed the trial court's dismissal. In the Fourth Circuit's opinion, the record contained "ample evidence from which the school officials could reasonably forecast that all of these Confederate flag shirts would materially and substantially disrupt the work and discipline of the school."[89] The court rejected Candice's argument that the Confederate flag shirts had in fact created no disruptions at LSD. "That the shirts never caused a disruption is not the issue," the court explained. "[R]ather the issue is whether school officials could reasonably forecast a disruption because of her shirts."[90]

Similarly, the appellate court rejected Candice's argument that the shirts merely symbolized her heritage and religious faith. "Again," the court reiterated, "the proper focus is whether school officials could predict that the Confederate flag shirts would cause a disruption."[91]

Finally, the court wrapped up its First Amendment analysis by ruling that school authorities reasonably predicted that one of her protest shirts—a shirt depicting the American flag along with the words "Old Glory" and "Flew over legalized slavery for 90 years!"—was likely to cause a substantial disruption even though the shirt did not display the Confederate flag.[92] The court also ruled that the school district's speech codes were not unconstitutionally vague or overbroad.

The *Hardwick* decision is notable because the Fourth Circuit ruled that the Latta School District reasonably anticipated that Candice's Confederate-flag depictions could cause a substantial disruption at school even though her controversial shirts, worn over a period of three school years, apparently caused no disruptions. In addition, the court found one of Candice's T-shirt carried the potential for disruption even though it did not display a Confederate flag.

One interesting aspect of the Confederate flag cases is the odd alliances that the Confederate-flag controversies have formed. The American Civil Liberties Union and the Sons of Confederate Veterans, as well as

Southern Legal Resource Center, have joined in opposing the school bans on Confederate symbols. "Though such groups fall on squarely opposite sides of the political spectrum," one commentator observed, "they are unified by their concern that student free speech is eroding and *Tinker*'s original principles are slowly unraveling with each decision upholding such bans."[93]

However, a strong trend has emerged toward banning the Confederate flag from school campuses. In the legal debate about whether Confederate images are symbols of heritage or symbols of oppression, the courts have generally concluded that the Confederate flag symbolizes racial oppression, which can lead to disruption.[94]

Moreover, regarding the fact that many students may wish to display a Confederate flag as a symbol of Southern heritage and not to communicate racial animus, most courts have concluded that schools still have the authority to ban their presence on school grounds. As a Sixth Circuit judge observed in one of these cases, "even if [an] individual student meant no hostility or contempt, a school administrator cannot practically administer a rule that permits such clothing sometimes and prohibits it other times depending on the intent of each individual wearer."[95] We agree.

CONCLUSION

All the cases discussed in this chapter have one common element; the federal courts looked to Supreme Court precedent for guidance when determining whether school authorities can constitutionally censor a particular student's clothing-borne expression. In most cases, the courts applied the Supreme Court's *Tinker* decision to the facts of their cases, asking whether school authorities reasonably anticipated that a particular student expression might cause a substantial disruption in the school setting. In some cases, the courts looked to *Fraser* and asked whether student expression was vulgar, plainly offensive, or contrary to the educational mission of the school. In one case, a court looked to *Morse v Frederick* for guidance in a clothing-based student expression case, but the overwhelming majority of student free speech cases involving messages on student clothing are decided under the principles laid down in *Tinker* or *Fraser*.

Recent cases indicate that federal courts are increasingly unsympathetic to students who claim a constitutional right to wear Confederate flags on their clothing while at school, and they have upheld school bans on Confederate regalia on various grounds. For example, the concurring opinion in *Defoe ex rel. Defoe v. Spiva* analogized *Morse*'s ban on student drug speech to racial divisiveness in a Confederate flag dress-code case. "If we substitute 'racial conflict' or 'racial hostility' for 'drug abuse,'" the concurring judge wrote, "the analysis in *Morse* is practically on all fours."[96]

Obviously, school districts would do well to have student dress codes that articulate the free speech standards laid out in the Supreme Court's decisions on students' free speech rights.

- Pursuant to *Tinker*, school policy should include a statement that the school can censor student expression that might reasonably be foreseen to create a substantial disruption in the school environment.
- Pursuant to *Fraser*, the school should reserve the right to ban student expression that is lewd, profane, indecent, or plainly offensive or that contains sexual innuendo.
- Pursuant to *Morse*, policy should prohibit student expression that celebrates or promotes the use of alcohol or the illegal use of drugs.

Readers who have reached the end of this chapter may conclude that a school-uniform policy or a tightly drafted dress code that prohibits all messages on students' clothing might make sense. In fact, the federal courts have given good guidance in several cases on the constitutionality of uniform codes and dress codes that prohibit almost all student messages. Those cases will be taken up in a companion volume.

NOTES

1. Robert J. Bein, "Stained Flag: Public Symbols and Equal Protection," 28 *Seton Hall Law Review* 897, 913 (1998).
2. Charlotte Brunel, *The T-Shirt Book* (New York: Assouline, 2002), 112; Alice Harris, *The White T* (New York: Harper Style, 1996), 44.
3. 286 F. Supp. 2d 847 (E.D. Mich. 203).
4. Ibid., 859.
5. Ibid., 857.
6. Guiles v. Marineau, 461 F.3d 320 (2d Cir. 2006).
7. Ibid., 322.
8. Ibid.
9. The Williamstown Middle / High School dress code reads: "Any aspect of a person's appearance, which constitutes a real hazard to the health and safety of self and others or is otherwise distracting, is unacceptable as an expression of personal taste. Example [C]lothing displaying alcohol, drugs, violence, obscenity, and racism is outside our responsibility and integrity as a school community and is prohibited." Ibid.
10. Ibid., 328.
11. Ibid., 329.
12. Brandt v. Board of Education of City of Chicago, 480 F.3d 460, 463 (7th Cir. 2007).
13. Ibid., 465.
14. 307 F.3d 243 (10th Cir. 2002).
15. Ibid., 255.
16. Ibid., 256.
17. Ibid., 257.

18. 421 F. Supp. 3d 410, 411 (D.N.H. 2006).

19. Ibid., 411.

20. Ibid., 414.

21. Ibid., 424.

22. 510 F. Supp. 2d 425 (S.D. Tex. 2007).

23. Ibid., 435.

24. Ibid., 436 (italics by the court).

25. 822 F. Supp. 2d 1037 (N.D. Cal. 2011).

26. The Fifth of May commemorates the Mexican army's 1862 victory over France in the Battle of Puebla during the Franco-Mexican War (1861–1867). It is a minor holiday in Mexico but it has evolved into a celebration of Mexican culture and heritage in the United States. Available at http://www.history.com/topics/cinco-de-mayo.

27. Dariano v. Morgan Hill Unified School District, 822 F. Supp. 2d at 1044.

28. Ibid., 1045.

29. Dariano v. Morgan Hill Unified School District, No. 11-17858 (9th Cir. Feb. 27, 2014) at *9 (citing to Karp v. Becken, 477 F.2d 171, 175 (9th Cir. 1973). The court noted that the school administrators had not instituted a blanket ban on American flag apparel, instead distinguishing between perceived levels of threat as a basis for action. Ibid., *11.

30. 220 F.3d 465 (6th Cir. 2000).

31. Ibid., 467.

32. Ibid., 466.

33. Ibid., 467.

34. Ibid.

35. Ibid., 469.

36. Ibid.

37. Ibid.

38. Ibid.

39. Ibid., 471.

40. Griggs v. Fort Wayne School Board, 359 F. Supp. 2d 731, 732-733 (N.D. Ind. 2005). The creed states in part:

My Rifle
The Creed of a United States Marine
This is my rifle. There are many like it, but this one is
mine. My rifle is my best friend. It is my life.
I must master it as I must master my life.
My rifle, without me, is useless. Without my rifle, I am
useless. I must fire my rifle true. I must shoot
straighter than my enemy who is trying to kill me. I
must shoot him before he shoots me. I will . . . (emphasis in original)
For the complete Creed written by Major General W.H. Rupertus following the attack on Pearl Harbor, access http://www.arlingtoncemetery.net/whruper.htm.

41. "The Board's principal argument is that, in the wake of tragic school shootings at Columbine High School and elsewhere, it has a 'legitimate pedagogical interest' in discouraging a 'culture of violence.'" Ibid., 744.

42. Ibid., 743.

43. Ibid.

44. "The Board's principal argument is that, in the wake of tragic school shootings at Columbine High School and elsewhere, it has a 'legitimate pedagogical interest' in discouraging a 'culture of violence.'" Ibid., 744.

45. Ibid., 748.

46. 354 F.3d 249 (4th Cir. 2003).

47. Ibid., 252.

48. Ibid.

49. Ibid.

50. Ibid., 253.

51. Ibid., 259–60.
52. Ibid., 260.
53. 588 F. Supp. 2d 606 (E.D. Penn. 2008).
54. Ibid., 611.
55. Ibid., 615.
56. Ibid., 618.
57. 551 U.S. 393 (2007).
58. Ibid., 625.
59. Williams v. Spencer, 622 F.2d 1200, 1205 (4th Cir. 1980).
60. Gano v. School District No. 411 of Twin Falls City, 674 F. Supp. 796 (D. Idaho 1987).
61. Ibid., 797.
62. Ibid., 798.
63. Edgar Dyer, "The Banning of Confederate Symbols in the Public Schools: Preventing Disruption or Avoiding Discomfort," 125, *Education Law Reporter* 1019, 1029 (1998).
64. For an early case involving the wearing of clothing depicting the Confederate flag to school, *see* Melton v. Young, 465 F.2d 1332 (6th Cir. 1972), in which an appellate court held that a school could reasonably forecast that wearing a jacket to school with the emblem of the Confederate flag would cause a material disruption. However, *see* Banks v. Muncie Community Schools, 433 F.2d 292 (7th Cir. 1970), in which the Seventh Circuit Court of Appeals upheld a school-district policy that allowed students of a new school in Muncie, Indiana, to vote on their symbols and mascot. The students voted for the Rebels and selected a symbol that resembled the Confederate flag. Suit was brought alleging that the symbols were inflammatory and discouraged Africa American students from participating in extracurricular activities. The federal district court found no racial discrimination but characterized the matter as "tyranny by the majority." The plaintiff also lost on appeal. The Court of Appeals found the symbols "offensive and that good policy would dictate their removal." Ibid., 299. However, the court did not find a constitutional violation and opined that the Board policy of allowing students to make choices allowed that they would make good choices as well bad choices.
65. 206 F.3d 1358 (10th Cir. 2000).
66. Ibid., 1362.
67. Ibid., 1366 (quoting the federal district trial court).
68. West v. Derby Unified School District #260, 23 F. Supp. 2d 1223, 1233 (D. Kan. 1998).
69. 324 F.3d 1246 (11th Cir. 2003).
70. Ibid., 1249 (internal citations and quotation marks omitted).
71. Ibid.
72. 538 F.3d 554, 557 (6th Cir. 2008).
73. Ibid., 557.
74. Ibid., 574.
75. Ibid., 567 (internal quotation marks omitted).
76. Ibid.
77. 554 F.3d 734 (8th Cir. 2009). Farmington High School had a predominately white student population of approximately 1,100 with only fifteen to twenty of those students African American.
78. Ibid., 736. The black student withdrew and attended another school.
79. Ibid.
80. 585 F.2d 214 (5th Cir. 2009).
81. Ibid., 222.
82. Ibid.
83. 711 F.3d 426 (4th Cir. 2013).
84. Ibid., 438.
85. Ibid., 430.

86. Ibid.

87. Ibid.

88. Ibid., 432.

89. Ibid., 438 (internal citations and quotation marks omitted).

90. Ibid., 439.

91. Ibid.

92. Ibid., 440.

93. Lucinda Housley Luetkemeyer, "Silencing the Rebel Yell: The Eighth Circuit Upholds a Public School's Ban on the Confederate Flags," 75, *Missouri Law Review* 989, 1007 (2010).

94. Dress codes targeting the Confederate battle flag are not the only retrenchment in the symbol of the "Old South." There is a decided movement toward removing Confederate mascots from public schools. For example, after a principal in Fairfax, Virginia, decided to ban the school's Confederate flag logo, the caricature "Johnny Reb," and the team name, the "Rebels," suit was brought by students. The principal banned the symbols even though there was no history of disruption associated with the symbols. The Fourth Circuit in a second appellate hearing upheld the decision to eliminate the Confederate symbols. The court concluded that school officials "have the authority to disassociate the school from controversial speech even if it may limit student expression" (Crosby v. Holsinger, 852 F.2d 801, 802 (4th Cir.1988). A school, over the objection of its students, may choose the symbols that it wants associated with its name.

95. Defoe ex rel. Defoe v. Spiva, 625 F.3d 324, 339 (6th Cir. 2010) (Roger, J. concurring).

96. Ibid., 339.

FIVE

Clothing Messages about Sex, Abortion, and Sexual Orientation

It is well understood that the right of free speech is not absolute at all times and under all circumstances.

—Chaplinsky v. New Hampshire [1]

As we saw in the previous chapter, students who come to school displaying messages on their clothing about politics, guns, drugs, and the Confederacy are likely to create some discomfort in the school community. After all, many people hold strong views on such issues as gun ownership, illegal drugs, and antebellum racial attitudes; and students who promote their own political views on such controversial issues while at school are sure to trigger a negative reaction from at least some people.

But sensitive as political issues are when discussed in a school, sexual issues are even more sensitive. It should not be surprising to find a significant number of court cases involving students who wish to proclaim messages about sex, abortion, and sexual orientation on their clothing. Thus, we have devoted a chapter to student clothing messages on sexual topics, which we have organized into three sections: clothing messages that are lewd, vulgar, or contain sexual innuendo; student clothing messages on abortion; and clothing-borne messages on sexual orientation.

CLOTHING MESSAGES THAT ARE LEWD, VULGAR OR CONTAIN SEXUAL INNUENDO

As every high school teacher or parent of a teenager knows, adolescents are afflicted with raging hormones, causing many of them to seem obsessively focused on sex. Their oral language is often laced with sexual innuendo and sexually explicit comments. Occasionally, students have

81

proclaimed sexual messages on their clothing and have sued school districts that have tried to censor such messages.

School authorities have clear legal guidance when a student communicates a sexual message at school that is lewd, vulgar, or indecent. As discussed in the second chapter, the Supreme Court said clearly in the case of *Bethel School District No. 403 v. Fraser* that schools can ban student speech that fits in these categories.[2]

This principle is illustrated in *Pyle v. South Hadley School Committee*, which concerns Jeffrey Pyle and his brother Jonathan, both students at South Hadley High School in Massachusetts, who wore T-shirts during the 1993–1994 school year that displayed messages that school administrators considered vulgar.[3] One T-shirt proclaimed, "See Dick Drink. See Dick Drive. See Dick Die. Don't be a Dick." Another shirt said this: "Coed Naked Band: Do it to the Rhythm." In addition, the brothers wore other T-shirts to school with provocative messages and sexual themes.

School authorities banned some of the Pyle brothers' T-shirt messages on the grounds that they violated the school district's dress code, and the brothers sued. They alleged a violation of their right to free speech under the First Amendment and asked a federal court to enjoin school officials from prohibiting them from wearing their sex-themed T-shirts.

A Massachusetts federal trial court acknowledged the seemingly trivial nature of the case, describing it as a "tempest in a teapot," but he took the dispute seriously, conducting a four-day trial on the merits of the Pyle brothers' claims. In the end, the court denied the Pyle brothers' request for an injunction and upheld the school district's decision to ban two of the brothers' T-shirts. In the court's view, the school board, not a federal judge, should determine "when the pungency of sexual foolery becomes unacceptable."[4] The court, did, however, invalidate one portion of the school district's speech code that prohibited student speech that was intended to harass individuals.

The Supreme Court's decision in *Fraser*, upholding a school's authority to ban lewd and vulgar speech in the school environment, was the principle case the federal court relied on when it upheld the South Hadley school committee's ban on the Pyle brothers' T-shirt messages. Today, most school districts have explicit policies banning lewd and vulgar speech at school, relying on the *Fraser* decision to support their position.

Often, it is an easy call for a court to determine that a particular student communication is vulgar and thus capable of being banned by school authorities under the rule laid down by *Fraser*. For example, in *Broussard v. School Board of the City of Norfolk*, a federal judge upheld a school's decision to prohibit Kimberly Broussard, a middle school girl, from wearing a T-shirt to school that proclaimed, "Drugs Suck!"[5]

The court concluded that school officials' determination "that the word 'suck' in the context of Kimberly's shirt is lewd, vulgar, or offensive is not merely a prudish failure to distinguish the vigorous from the vulgar, but rather is a permissible decision by the school to regulate middle school children's language and channel their expression into socially appropriate speech."[6] In the court's view, the word "suck" clearly had a sexual connotation, even though the word was sometimes used merely as an expression of disapproval.

Sometimes, however, it is not easy to determine whether a particular student message is vulgar. For example, in *B.H. v. Easton Area School District*, a 2011 case, officials at a Pennsylvania school district sanctioned two middle school girls who refused to remove bracelets proclaiming the message "I ♥ Boobies" as part of a campaign to promote breast-cancer awareness.[7] The school district asserted that it had the right to prohibit the wearing of the bracelets under *Fraser*, which restricts student speech that is lewd, vulgar, profane, or plainly offensive. The girls sued, claiming a violation of their right to free speech.

A federal trial court ruled in the girls' favor. The court concluded that the phrase "boobies" in the context of a communication on the importance of breast-cancer awareness had no sexual connotation and was not lewd or vulgar, and thus the bracelets could not be banned on that basis.

The school also argued that the bracelets would likely create a substantial disruption in the school environment, pointing out that the bracelets had led to some inappropriate remarks by middle school boys. But the court rejected this argument as well. "Such isolated incidents," the court noted, "are well within a school's ability to maintain discipline and order and they did not because a disruption to the School's learning environment."[8]

The school district appealed and the case was heard by the Third Circuit of Appeals, sitting *en banc*.[9] In a split decision, the appellate court upheld the district court's decision, finding the school district's prohibition of the bracelets violated the female students' constitutional rights. The court held that the "I ♥ Boobies" bracelets were not plainly lewd and that they expressed support for an important national social issue— breast cancer awareness. Therefore, the bracelet could not be categorically restricted. Essentially, the court ruled that ambiguously lewd speech that plausibly comments on political or social issues is deserving of protection.

Judge Hardiman, dissenting, offered a critique of the majority view that ambiguously lewd speech that comments on a political or social issue should be constitutionally protected. He asked whether middle school students, under the majority's ruling, should be allowed to wear bracelets to school that proclaimed the message "feelmyballs.org" if the bracelets were worn in support of the Testicular Cancer Awareness Project.

On the other hand, a federal court in Wisconsin, ruling on similar facts, denied a middle school student's request for an injunction that would permit them to wear "I ♥ Boobies" bracelets at school.[10] "In this court's opinion," the court wrote, "[t]he statement 'I ♥ Boobies! (Keep a Breast)' straddles the line between vulgar and mildly inappropriate."[11] Thus, the court explained, it was reasonable for school officials to conclude that the phrase was vulgar "and inconsistent with their goal of fostering respectful discourse by encouraging students to use 'correct anatomical terminology' for human body parts."[12]

In a similar ruling, a federal judge in Indiana ruled that the Fort Wayne School District could ban "I ♥ Boobies! (Keep a Breast)" bracelets, pointedly declining to follow the Third Circuit's ruling in *B.H.*[13] There was no showing of disruption caused by the bracelet, the Indiana federal judge acknowledged. In banning the bracelets, the school district relied on *Fraser*, arguing that the ban was aimed at stopping lewd and vulgar speech in the school environment.

The judge deferred to the judgment of educators with regard to deciding what kind of speech is inappropriate at school. "Judges are 'outsiders,'" the court wrote, "who do not have the experience and competence to tell school authorities how to run schools in a way that will preserve an atmosphere conducive to learning."[14] Accordingly, the court refused to issue an injunction stopping the implementation of the bracelet ban, which it believed would "take away the deference courts owe to schools and make their job much harder."[15]

The conflict among courts about the appropriateness of "I ♥ Boobies!" bracelets in a public school does not change that fact that overall, courts and school officials will usually agree with regard to what types of student expressions are vulgar, lewd, or indecent. Certainly, almost all reasonable judges would agree that "Drugs Suck!" and "Don't Be a Dick" are offensive phrases in the school environment and can be banned without violating a student's free speech rights under the First Amendment.

STUDENTS WHO PROCLAIM THEIR OPPOSITION TO ABORTION ON THEIR CLOTHING

Perhaps no social issue is more divisive or inspires more militant advocates than abortion. Not surprisingly, debates about abortion have sparked litigation in the education sector—both at the K–12 level and in the universities. For example, in *Pro-Life Cougars v. University of Houston*,[16] a public university in Texas attempted to relegate an anti-abortion student group's pro-life photographic exhibit to an out-of-the-way spot on campus rather than a more visible location, based on the unilateral conclusion by the Dean of Students that the pro-life display was "potentially disruptive." A federal court ruled that the university had violated the group's constitutional rights.

For an opposite finding on the issue of disruption, the Tenth Circuit Court of Appeals addressed the free speech rights of several students who were members of a religious youth group called "Relentless."[17] The students planned, without permission, to pass out 2,500 rubber fetus dolls at their high school. The dolls had a card affixed to them with a statement that the dolls represented the actual size and weight of a 12-week-old fetus. On the other side of the card was a religious message.[18]

The relentless students offered a fetus to students who were passing by their display table but allowed students to decline and move along. There was no blockage of the entrance to the school where they set up their distribution table. The assistant principal shut down the distribution after approximately three hundred dolls were distributed. The assistant principal noticed that several students were throwing the dismembered heads of the dolls against walls.

At the trial, the plaintiff students argued that the "disruptions occurred only because of the behavior of third parties, that no plaintiffs had participated in these activities,"[19] and that no substantial disruption had occurred. The court disagreed, citing *Tinker* for the proposition that school authorities need not tolerate speech they reasonably believe might cause a disruption. "[T]he District was not obligated to wait until a substantial disruption materialized," the court ruled, "so long as its forecast was reasonable."[20]

In at least two court cases, federal judges have been called on to decide whether a student in a public high school has a constitutional right to express opposition to abortion on the student's T-shirt. In *K.D. v. Fillmore Central School District*,[21] K.D., a sophomore, repeatedly came to school wearing a provocative pro-life T-shirt. In capital letters, the front of the shirt proclaimed: "ABORTION IS HOMICIDE." The back of the shirt expressed this message:

> You will not silence my message.
> You will not mock my God.
> You will stop killing my generation.
> Rock for Life![22]

K.D.'s school had a dress-code policy, which required students to wear clothing that is "appropriate and [does] not disrupt or interfere with the educational process."[23] At first, principal Kyle Faulkner, took a low-key approach to K.D's T-shirts, simply asking K.D. to "do him a favor" and refrain from wearing the shirt to school.[24]

However, Faulkner later received complaints from female students about K.D.'s T-shirt. One student said the T-shirt upset her and that she did not "want to be near [K.D.] or anywhere near that shirt."[25] The principal also knew that there were female students in the school who had had abortions or who were contemplating an abortion, and he concluded that each such student "would consider the shirt to be a personal attack on her, but that each girl would not likely come forward to complain."[26]

Finally, on an October school day, Faulkner told K.D. the shirt was not appropriate for school and asked him to cover the shirt's message, turn the shirt inside out or wear a different shirt. Faulkner gave K.D. the choice of changing his attire or going home for the day. K.D. refused to change his shirt, and he left school.

K.D. sued the school district, alleging a violation of his First Amendment right to free expression. Before a federal judge, K.D. sought a court order directing school officials not to interfere with his right to wear his "ABORTON IS HOMICIDE" T-shirt to school.

School defendants made four arguments in support of their contention that they properly banned K.D.'s T-shirt: First, they claimed K.D.'s T-shirt message was factually inaccurate because it claims that abortion is homicide. Since abortion is legal, the school authorities, reasoned, it is not the unlawful taking of life. Second, the defendants argued the T-shirt was a direct attack on students who had had an abortion or were contemplating an abortion and that such attacks are inappropriate in the school. Third, they maintained that abortion is a subject that is frequently associated with violence and could be banned on that basis. Finally, Principal Faulkner and the school district contended that abortion is a topic to which elementary students should not be exposed.

In connection with their last argument, the defendants pointed out that K.D. attended a school where students from pre-kindergarten to twelfth grade were housed in one building. They submitted statements from several parents of elementary students who asserted they did not want their children exposed to the topic of abortion.

A federal district judge rejected all of these arguments and sided with K.D. In the judge's opinion, K.D. had engaged in passive political speech that had been censored because of its content. The judge said there was insufficient evidence to show that K.D.'s T-shirt had disrupted the school environment and no evidence showing that an elementary school child had actually seen the shirt. Moreover, it was simply incorrect to say that K.D.'s shirt consisted of a personal attack on students who had had abortions. "That a student may have an opposing view does not make K.D.'s T-shirt a personal attack on that student for having an opposing viewpoint," the judge reasoned.[27]

Based on these considerations, the judge granted K.D.'s request for an injunction. The Fillmore Central School District was prohibited from requiring K.D. to remove, turn inside out, or cover the message on his T-shirt, the court ordered, unless it could show that KD.'s "ABORTION IS HOMICIDE" T-shirt had caused or was likely to cause "a material or substantial disruption of the orderly administration of the school."[28]

Another federal court, this one in California, ruled very differently from the ruling in *K.D. v. Fillmore Central School District*. In *T.A. v. McSwain Elementary School*,[29] a case involving facts similar to the *Fillmore* case, a trial court denied a student's request for an order permitting her to wear an anti-abortion T-shirt to school.

In the *McSwain* case, a sixth grader wore a T-shirt to school that featured the word "ABORTION" on the front side. Below the word were three squares approximately three inches in height. The first two squares depicted color images of a human fetus in two stages of development. "The third square—containing no image—is filled in with black." Below the three squares, these words appeared: "growing, growing . . . gone."[30]

The back of the shirt proclaimed this message:

American Life League's
Sixth Annual
NATIONAL
PRO-LIFE
T-SHIRT-DAY
APRIL 29, 2008 www.ALL.org[31]

T.A.'s school had a dress and grooming policy that prohibited students from wearing clothing that "present[s] a health or safety hazard or a distraction which would interfere with the educational process."[32] The school also had a "Freedom of Speech/Expression Policy" that prohibited student speech that causes a "substantial disruption of the school's orderly operation."[33]

A teacher spotted T.A. wearing her pro-life T-shirt while eating breakfast at the school. She was taken to the school office, where C. W. Smith, the assistant principal, determined that the shirt violated the school's dress-code policy. T.A. was given a temporary T-shirt to wear, and she filed a lawsuit.

In responding to T.A's motion for an injunction, the school defended its decision to ban T.A.'s shirt on two grounds. First, assistant principal Smith determined the pictures on T.A.'s T-shirt were "too graphic for the younger students that we have at our school site."[34]

Second, as it happened, T.A. had worn the T-shirt to school during the week that children were taking the STAR test, a state-mandated standardized test. Smith feared the pictures on T.A.'s shirt "would distract students during the time in which they should have been taking the STAR test."[35]

In denying T.A.'s motion for summary judgment on her constitutional claims, the court issued findings favorable to the school district. "Defendants have presented evidence," the court ruled, "that the restriction imposed on [T.A.] was not based on the viewpoint expressed by [T.A's] shirt, but rather on the graphic pictures contained on it."[36] In addition, the court ruled, "Defendants have presented evidence that based on their experience and judgment, they believed the shirt would have created a substantial disruption of or a material interference with school activities, especially in the context of the standardized testing being administered at the school on the day in question."[37]

Besides her First Amendment claim, T.A. presented two other constitutional arguments. She claimed the school's dress code was unconstitutionally vague, in violation of substantive due process; and she argued she had been denied equal protection in that the school censored her pro-life message while permitting other views on abortion to be expressed. The court was not persuaded by either argument. In the court's view, the school's policy passed constitutional muster on the vagueness issue. Regarding T.A.'s equal protection argument, the court said the claim that she had been treated differently based on her views would have to be determined after a trial.

T.A. v. McSwain Union Elementary School and *K.D. v. Fillmore Central School District* involve similar facts, but the outcomes were different. Indeed, it is interesting to note that K.D.'s T-shirt's rather militant message that "ABORTION IS HOMICIDE" was ruled nondisruptive while T.A.'s much milder message was viewed as one that could disrupt a school's testing program. It seems likely that the temperament and dispositions of the ruling judges explain the contrary rulings as much as any distinctions in the facts of the case or judicial interpretations of the law.

CLOTHING MESSAGES ABOUT SEXUAL ORIENTATION AND SEXUALITY

A second type of sexual themed student-clothing message pertains to student expressions about sexuality and sexual orientation. Usually, students who make pronouncements on the topic of sexual orientation are not doing so to be vulgar or bawdy. Instead, students who proclaim messages on this topic usually do so as a way of communicating their political or religious views.

It seems clear that students have the right to proclaim their support for gay and lesbian students while at school so long as their expressions are not disruptive, lewd, or in violation of a valid dress code. For example, in *Gillman v. School Board of Holmes County*, high school students in a Florida school district publicly displayed their support for "Jane Doe," a lesbian classmate, after the school principal allegedly harassed Jane because of her sexual orientation.[38] Incorrectly concluding that the principal had suspended Jane, students expressed support for her by writing "GP" or "Gay Pride" on their bodies, wearing T-shirts proclaiming their support for gay rights, shouting "Gay Pride" in the school hallways, or creating signs expressing support for homosexuals.

At some point in this controversy, the principal suspended eleven students for their participation in the so-called Gay Pride movement. The principal interviewed approximately thirty students about the "Gay

Pride" activities, questioning them about their sexual orientation and about their involvement in the planned walkout at a school assembly. He prohibited students from wearing rainbow belts or writing "Gay Pride" or "GP" on their arms and notebooks.[39]

In light of the principal's prohibition of messages expressing support for homosexuals, one student, Heather Gillman sought clarification from the school board regarding such messages. Specifically, she sought permission from the school board to display various gay-friendly messages, including one proclaiming, "I Support My Gay Friends."

The school board responded to Heather in a letter stating that none of the gay-friendly messages she had proposed could be displayed at school. The school board justified its prohibition by claiming that the messages were an indication of membership in an "illegal organization" prohibited by school policy and that the messages were disruptive to the educational process.[40]

Via her mother, Heather sued the school district, claiming that its policies against student expression in support of gay rights violated the First Amendment. The school board responded by arguing that the pro-gay messages could foreseeably cause substantial disruption at the school and therefore could be banned under *Tinker*. Indeed, at trial, the principal testified that students should not be permitted to wear political buttons expressing support for presidential candidates while at school because such expressions might cause "controversy" and "unrest."[41]

A Florida federal trial judge rejected the school district's justification for banning pro-gay messages and ruled in Heather's favor. The court noted that the facts of the case were extraordinary: "The Holmes County School Board has imposed an outright ban on speech by students that is not vulgar, lewd, obscene, plainly offensive, or violent, but which is pure, political, and expresses tolerance, acceptance, fairness, and support for not only a marginalized group, but more importantly, for a fellow student at Ponce de Leon [High School]."[42] This kind of speech, the judge emphasized, is exactly the kind of speech that "is essential in a vibrant, progressive society and is precisely the type of speech that is sacrosanct under the First Amendment."[43]

The court emphatically rejected the school district's argument that the pro-gay messages would likely lead to disruption, concluding that the examples of disruption the district put forward were "speculative, theoretical, and de minimis."[44]

Although a student's First Amendment right to express tolerance and support for homosexuals seems well established, a student's constitutional right to express disapproval of homosexuality at school is less clear. One of the most important federal court opinions on this topic is *Harper v. Poway Unified School District*,[45] in which the Ninth Circuit Court of Appeals ruled that there is no such right; but other courts have disagreed with the *Harper* court's analysis.

In *Harper*, school officials at Poway High School permitted the Gay-Straight Alliance, a student group, to sponsor a "Day of Silence" at the school to promote tolerance toward Gays and Lesbians.[46] Tye Harper, a high school student, disagreed with the theme of the Day of Silence. On the appointed date for the Day of Silence, he wore a T-shirt expressing his view that homosexual conduct is sinful from a Christian perspective.

The front of Harper's T-shirt proclaimed this message: "I WILL NOT ACCEPT WHAT GOD HAS CONDEMNED." The back of his shirt communicated a similar message: "'HOMOSEXUALITY IS SHAMEFUL' - Romans 1:27."[47]

Apparently, school authorities did not see Harper's T-shirt, and nothing was said to him about it. The following day, however, Harper came to school wearing the same T-shirt, which was emblazoned with an additional message: "BE ASHAMED, OUR SCHOOL EMBRACED WHAT GOD HAS CONDEMNED."[48]

A teacher confronted Harper about the shirt, but Harper refused to take it off. The teacher gave Harper a dress code violation card and sent him to the front office. At the front office, the principal told Tye that he considered the T-shirt's messages to be inflammatory and that it was the school's "intent to avoid physical conflict on campus." The principal also expressed the view "that it was not healthy for students to be addressed in such a derogatory manner."[49]

Tye refused to remove the T-shirt. Although he twice requested to be suspended, the principal did not suspend him or discipline him. Instead, he required Tye to remain in the front office until the end of the school day.

Tye Harper sued the school district, alleging a violation of his First Amendment right to free speech. His case was dismissed by a federal trial court on the grounds that Tye's T-shirt messages could foreseeably cause a substantial disruption at his school and thus could be banned under *Tinker*. Tye then appealed to the Ninth Circuit Court of Appeals. In a decision issued in April of 2006, a three-judge panel of the Ninth Circuit upheld the trial court, with one judge dissenting.

In ruling for the school district, the Ninth Circuit articulated an expansive interpretation of the Supreme Court's *Tinker* decision, an interpretation that surprised many legal commentators all over the United States. In its decision, the court affirmed *Tinker*'s principle that schools can ban student speech that could foreseeably cause a "substantial disruption" in the school environment. This, of course, had been the standard interpretation of *Tinker* by the federal courts for decades and was in no way surprising.

Remarkably, however, the Ninth Circuit focused on a passage in *Tinker* that had generally been overlooked by both courts and scholars. In addition to student speech that causes or is likely to cause a substantial disruption, the Ninth Circuit pointed out, the Supreme Court also said that schools can censor student speech that "intrudes upon . . . the rights of other students" or "collides with the rights of students to be secure and left alone.'"[50]

In the Ninth Circuit's opinion, Tye Harper's anti-gay T-shirt messages "collide[d] with the rights of other students in the most fundamental way."[51] The court rejected the argument of Tye's counsel that *Tinker* only intended to protect students from physical confrontations. On the contrary, the court said, "Public school students who may be injured by verbal assaults on the basis of a core identifying characteristic such as race, religion, or sexual orientation, have a right to be free from such attacks while on school campuses."[52] The right to be secure while at school, the Ninth Circuit emphasized, included "not only freedom from physical assaults but from psychological attacks that cause young people to question their self-worth and their rightful place in society."[53]

In the Ninth Circuit's view, student speech that demeaned gay and lesbian students was "detrimental not only to their psychological health and well-being, but also to their educational development."[54] Thus, it is well established, the court said, that attacks on students based on sexual orientation were "harmful not only to the students' health and welfare, but also to their educational performance and their ultimate potential for success in life."[55]

The Ninth Circuit affirmed *Tinker*'s holding that student speech cannot be suppressed simply because some people find it offensive. It pointed out that a student may have a constitutional right to say, "Young Republicans Suck," or "Young Democrats Suck." But—in the Ninth Circuit's view at least—schools do not offend the First Amendment by banning students from engaging in "derogatory and injurious remarks directed at students' minority status such as race, religion, and sexual orientation."[56]

Although the *Harper* decision has been widely criticized for attempting to cut back on *Tinker*'s robust affirmation of a student's right to free speech in the school environment, the court's reasoning makes sense to many people.[57] In particular, the following passage of the Ninth Circuit's opinion persuasively argues that demeaning speech directed toward vulnerable students can be harmful.

> Speech that attacks high school students who are members of minority groups that have been historically oppressed, subjected to verbal and physical abuse, and made to feel inferior, serves to injure and intimidate them, as well as to damage their sense of security and interfere with their opportunity to learn. The demeaning of young gay and lesbian students in a school environment is detrimental not only to their psychological health and wellbeing, but also to their educational development.[58]

Based on these considerations of harm, the Ninth Circuit made clear that school officials have the authority to ban student speech that targets at least three vulnerable groups of students—students targeted because of their race, sexual orientation, or religion. "Those who administer our public educational institutions," the court said emphatically, "need not tolerate verbal assaults that may destroy the self-esteem of our most vulnerable teenagers and interfere with their educational development."[59]

Interestingly, although the *Harper* decision inspired a lot of scholarly commentary, its reasoning has not been followed by all federal courts. In fact, in three cases—all involving anti-gay messages on student's T-shirts, federal courts upheld the right of students to proclaim their opposition to homosexuality, based on findings that the critical messages did not disrupt the school environment.

In *Chambers v. Babbitt*, decided several years before the Ninth Circuit's *Harper* decision was handed down, Elliott Chambers, a student at Woodbury High School in Minnesota, wore a sweatshirt to school that proclaimed the message "Straight Pride."[60] The back of the sweatshirt displayed the image of a man and woman holding hands. Elliott's promotion of heterosexuality and implicit condemnation of homosexuality were informed at least in part by his religious beliefs.

Elliott attended a Christian student group at the school and had used the group as a forum to share biblical passages supporting the claim that homosexuality is sinful.[61] In his testimony, he argued that the school was advocating homosexuality through its tolerance-promoting policies.[62] Thus, it appears that his sweatshirt served as a protest against the school's tolerance for nonheterosexual relationships.

At least one student complained to school authorities about the message on Elliott's sweatshirt, and the principal told him not to wear the shirt to school again.

Elliott sued, arguing that the principal's directive violated his constitutional right to express his religious beliefs. The court granted his request for an injunction prohibiting the school from banning Elliott's sweatshirt message unless it had a reasonable belief that Elliott's message could lead to substantial disruption of the school environment or material interference with school activities."[63]

In reaching its decision, the court in Elliott Chambers's case relied primarily on its interpretation of *Tinker*'s substantial disruption test. The school district maintained that Elliott's arguably anti-gay message could disrupt the school environment and cited evidence of eleven fights between students during the school year. The court was not persuaded, however, pointing out that the relationship between the fighting incidents and Elliott's sweatshirt had not been explained.

The court concluded its opinion with an observation about the importance of tolerance toward different points of view. "Our schools, like our communities at large, are invaluably improved by the diversity of their members," the court observed. "All students benefit from the respectful and thoughtful exchange of ideas and sharing of beliefs and practices." In the court's view, "[s]chools, in particular, are vital environments that can provide an education of both the substance of diversity and the responsible manner with which such diversity is approached and expressed."[64]

The court acknowledged that Elliott's "Straight Pride" sweatshirt message apparently expressed an intolerant attitude toward homosexuals. However, the court pointed out that tolerance includes tolerating viewpoints such as those expressed by "Straight Pride." Thus, the school had a responsibility "to maintain an environment open to diversity and to educate and support its students as they confront ideas different from their own."[65]

Nixon v. Northern Local School District, a 2005 opinion, expressed a similar point of view.[66] In this case, James Nixon, a middle school student in Licking County, Ohio, wore a T-shirt to school that contained religious messages and a disapproval of homosexuality. The front of the shirt proclaimed the word "INTOLERANT" with this added message: "Jesus said . . . I am the way, the truth and life." The back of the shirt displayed these words: "Homosexuality is a sin! Islam is a lie! Abortion is murder! Some issues are just black and white!"[67]

The school's guidance counselor spotted James wearing his controversial T-shirt and asked him to remove it or wear it turned inside out. James refused, and the counselor escorted him to the principal's office. At the principal's office, an assistant principal viewed James's shirt and concluded that it was offensive and in violation of school policy. Unless James removed the shirt or wore it turned inside out, the assistant principal told James, he would not be permitted to return to school.

At some point, James's father arrived at the school, where he supported his son's right to wear the anti-gay T-shirt. The father refused to leave the school until he received a satisfactory explanation as to why the shirt was offensive. School authorities called the sheriff's department. A deputy sheriff arrived and took the father's statement, whereupon James and the father left the school.

The school superintendent backed the principal regarding James's T-shirt and affirmed the principal's message that James would be suspended if he returned to school wearing the shirt. The superintendent agreed with the principal that James's shirt violated school policy, which stated that "[a]ny fashion (dress, accessory or hairstyle) that disrupts the education process . . . will not be permitted."[68]

In due course, James and his parents sued the school district, seeking an injunction that would bar school officials from prohibiting James from wearing his controversial T-shirt to school. Before the court, school defendants made two arguments in defense of the decision to ban the shirt on the school campus. First, relying on the *Tinker* decision, school officials argued that the T-shirt had the potential for causing disruption "based on the fact that the school includes students and/or staff members who are Muslims, homosexuals and those who have had abortions."[69] Second, the defendants maintained that James's messages were offensive and could be banned in accordance with the Supreme Court's *Fraser* decision.

A federal court rejected both of the school district's legal arguments and granted James's request for an injunction that would allow him to wear his T-shirt at school. With regard to the school's disruption argument, the court pointed out that there was no evidence that James's shirt had caused a disruption in the school environment or that his shirt was likely to cause a disruption. In the court's view, the mere fact that the school community contained people who were targets of James's messages (Muslims, homosexuals, and women who had had abortions) fell "well short of the *Tinker* standard for reasonably anticipating a disruption of school activities."[70]

Nor, in the court's opinion, could school officials ban James's shirt on the grounds that it was "plainly offensive" under *Fraser*. In the court's view, "plainly offensive" as the Supreme Court and other courts interpreted that phrase referred to speech that was vulgar, contained sexual innuendoes, or promoted suicide, drugs, alcohol or murder. Thus, the court concluded, a potentially offensive political speech such as the views expressed on James's T-shirt could not be categorized as "plainly offensive" for purposes of regulation in the school environment.

Although the court ruled in James Nixon's favor, it expressed sympathy for school officials who have the responsibility to maintain safe and orderly schools. "In light of the Columbine school shootings and other tragic attacks that have happened on school grounds, the Court wholly understand that school administrators and staff must be extra vigilant in protecting students," the court acknowledged. The court emphasized that its decision in favor of James's right to wear his controversial T-shirt was not "an admonishment of the well-intentioned actions school officials take to ensure a stable educational environment."[71]

Finally, in *Zamecnik v. Indian Prairie School District*, decided after the *Harper* decision, the Seventh Circuit Court of Appeals sided with students who were barred from wearing T-shirts to school that proclaimed "Be Happy, Not Gay," a phrase that expressed mild disapproval of homosexuality.[72] In a previous opinion, the Seventh Circuit had granted the students a preliminary injunction allowing them to wear the shirts, concluding that the shirt's message was "only tepidly negative" and finding no evidence that the shirts disrupted the school environment in any substantial way.[73]

In a later opinion, the Seventh Circuit affirmed a lower court order granting summary judgment to the students. At the appellate level, the school district had argued that the lower court had entered summary judgment prematurely, citing evidence that the T-shirts had in fact created a substantial disruption and presenting an expert witness's report that supported its position.

The Seventh Circuit found the school's evidence of disruption to be negligible and that some of the disruption consisted of a "heckler's veto," action or speech by people who opposed the T-shirt wearers' point of view. The court gave little credence to the school district's expert report, which contained no reference to the school where the T-shirts were worn. The court noted dryly that the majority of the thirty-eight-page report consisted of the expert's vita and that the substance of the report was only two-and-a-half pages long.

What do the cases tell us regarding whether students have the right to proclaim anti-gay messages on their clothing while at school? The *Harper* case states flatly that schools can prohibit these messages because they are harmful to vulnerable students. The *Zamecnik* case upheld the right of students to proclaim a mildly gay message—"Be happy, Not Gay"—on T-shirts but acknowledged that harsh anti-gay messages could be banned if they fell within the category of "fighting words."

It is interesting to note that in both the *Harper* case and the *Zamecnik* case, the plaintiff students wore anti-gay messages in response to school approved activities that supported tolerance toward gays and lesbians. In *Harper*, the Ninth Circuit upheld the Poway school district's ban on a student's anti-gay speech even though the school itself promoted an alternative point of view.

The Seventh Circuit disagreed with the Ninth Circuit on this important point. In the Seventh Circuit's view, "a school that permits advocacy of the rights of homosexual students cannot be allowed to stifle criticism of homosexuality."[74]

In our view, the Seventh Circuit's position is better reasoned than the Ninth Circuit's view. From the perspective of basic fairness, we do not believe a school district should take an aggressive position in favor of gay and lesbian rights while stifling student voices that disagree. As Judge Kozinski's dissenting opinion in *Harper* pointed out, it hardly seems fair for a school to introduce a controversial topic into the school environment and prohibit one point of view from being expressed in the marketplace of ideas.[75]

Of course, the restrictions of *Tinker* and *Fraser* should certainly apply with full force in such situations. Certainly, as the Seventh Circuit acknowledged, schools have the authority to censor anti-gay speech that is hateful or so incendiary that it constitutes fighting words, but a school that promotes tolerance for gays and lesbians should also be able to tolerate student speech that takes an opposite view—certainly speech that merely exhorts students to "Be Happy, Not Gay."

An area of potentially growing controversy for dress codes is transgendered students[76] and students who challenge gender-specific dress regulations. Dress-code restrictions that require that students wear gender conforming/appropriate attire have been coming under scrutiny. One commentator observed, "Sometimes, the challenges involve transgender students, but more frequently they involve students who simply have a different fashion sense from school administrators."[77] For example, an openly gay female student went to court and won the right to bring her same-sex partner to the prom and to wear a tuxedo to express her identity.[78]

DRESS CODES THAT PROHIBIT VIRTUALLY ALL MESSAGES ON STUDENT CLOTHING

In a 2009 decision entitled *Palmer v. Waxahachie Independent School District*, the Fifth Circuit Court of Appeals decided a case that may be a game changer with regard to student dress-code litigation.[79] In *Palmer*, the Fifth Circuit ruled that a Texas school district could bar a high school student from wearing a T-shirt or polo shirt that proclaimed *any* message other than a principal-approved message pertaining to school spirit, student clubs or athletic teams.[80]

The dispute between student Paul Palmer and the Waxahachie School District began when Palmer wore a T-shirt to school that simply proclaimed the words "San Diego." The principal told Palmer that the shirt's message violated the school district's dress code and told him to go home and return wearing another shirt. Palmer complied, but later he appeared at school wearing other messaged clothing, including two shirts supporting John Edwards for president of the United States and a T-shirt that displayed the language of the First Amendment.[81]

Without analyzing whether the shirts' messages might be disruptive under *Tinker*'s "substantial disruption" standard, the Fifth Circuit simply ruled that the school district's dress code was a content-neutral regulation and that the district had an important governmental interest in regulating students' clothing while they were at school.[82] The court used the intermediate scrutiny test of *United States v. O'Brien*,[83] a non-education case, for its analysis.

In concluding that the Waxahachie School District had a substantial governmental interest in its dress code, the Fifth Circuit cited the code's preamble, which stated that the code was adopted "to maintain an orderly and safe learning environment, increase the focus in instruction, promote safety and life-long learning, and encourage professional and responsible dress for all students."[84]

In the Fifth Circuit's view, "improving the educational process" was an important governmental interest,[85] as was "instilling self-confidence, increasing attendance, decreasing disciplinary referrals, and lowering the drop-out rate."[86] And the district had an important governmental interest in encouraging "professional dress" as well.[87] Finally, the court pointed out, "[T]he benefits for the school, such as reducing time spent enforcing the code and promoting school spirit, are also important in promoting better education."[88]

Significantly, the Fifth Circuit did not require the Waxahachie School District to provide quantitative evidence that its dress code actually furthered the interests that it articulated. "We do not . . . require statistical or scientific evidence to uphold a dress code," the court stated, noting that "improvements in discipline or morale cannot always be quantified."[89] In the Fifth Circuit's view, school authorities were in a better position than the courts to determine the benefits of a dress code.[90]

In short, the Fifth Circuit had no qualms about upholding a school district's dress code that banned all messages on students' shirts unless they pertained to school spirit, athletics, or school clubs. "[S]o long as a dress code does not restrict student dress outside of school and provides them with some means to communicate their speech during school," the court concluded, it passes constitutional muster.[91]

CONCLUSION

The preceding discussion and chapters 3 and 4 discussed dress codes that either target messages or reduce student speech by limiting students' choice of clothing. As we have seen, the courts do not always agree about which student messages can be banned by school authorities. Nevertheless, in particular, courts have disagreed about whether students can wear clothing to school that proclaims their opposition to homosexuality and abortion. In most cases, the courts have looked to *Tinker* when deciding whether a particular messaged item of clothing can be banned, asking whether the clothing disrupted the school environment or had the potential for creating a disruption.

Palmer v. Waxahachie Independent School District, decided by the Fifth Circuit in 2009, applied a different line of reasoning in upholding a school district's dress code that banned all messages on student clothing except for messages that were approved by the school principal and pertained to school spirit, school clubs, or athletics. Without looking to *Tinker*, the court concluded that the school district's dress code was content-neutral and advanced an important interest in maintaining a safe and orderly school environment. Importantly, the court did not require the school district to submit statistical evidence showing that the dress code did in fact promote safety and learning.

The *Palmer* case is in line with several federal decisions that have upheld school districts' school-uniform policies. In fact, as will be discussed more fully in a companion volume, so far the courts have generally ruled in favor of school districts when school-uniform policies were challenged by students on constitutional grounds.

The *Palmer* decision may be an indication that school districts can reduce their exposure to students' lawsuits challenging student dress codes if they adopt dress codes that ban *all* messages on student clothing, with the exception of messages pertaining to school activities that are pre-approved by school authorities. In other words, schools may stand a better chance of winning student dress-code lawsuits if they have a restrictive code in place that prohibits all nonapproved messages on clothing rather than a more permissive dress code that allows students to argue that their particular message is nondisruptive.

NOTES

1. Chaplinsky v. New Hampshire, 315 U.S. 568, 571–72 (1942).
2. 478 U.S. 675 (1986).
3. 861 F. Supp. 157 (D. Mass. 1994).
4. Ibid., 170.
5. 801 F. Supp. 1526 (E.D. Va. 1992).
6. Ibid., 1537 (internal citations and quotation marks omitted).
7. 827 F. Supp. 2d 392 (E.D. Pa. 2011).
8. Ibid., 409.
9. B.H. Easton v. Easton Area School District, 725 F.3d 293 (3d Cir. 2013).
10. K.J. v. Sauk Prairie School District, 11-cv-622-bbc, 2012 U.S. Dis. LEXIS 187689 (W.D. Wis. 2012).
11. Ibid., 17 (Lexis Nexis pagination).
12. Ibid., 22.
13. J.A. v. Fort Wayne Community Schools, 2013 U.S. Dist. LEXIS 117667 (N.D. Ind. 2013).
14. Ibid., 8 (LexisNexis pagination) (internal citations omitted).
15. Ibid., 20.
16. 259 F. Supp. 2d 575 (S.D. Tex. 2003).
17. Taylor v. Roswell Independent School District, 714 F.3d 25 (10th Cir.2013).
18. Ibid., 30.
19. Ibid., 38.
20. Ibid., 39.
21. 2005 U.S. Dist. LEXIS 33871 (W.D.N.Y. 2005).
22. Ibid., 3 (LexisNexis pagination).
23. Ibid.
24. Ibid., 4.
25. Ibid., 5.
26. Ibid.
27. Ibid., 16.
28. Ibid., 25.
29. T.A. v. McSwain Union Elementary School, 2010 U.S. Dist. LEXIS 71973 (E.D. Cal. 2010).
30. Ibid., 4 (LexisNexis pagination).
31. Ibid.
32. Ibid., 2.
33. Ibid., 3.
34. Ibid., 5
35. Ibid., 10.
36. Ibid.
37. Ibid., 11.

38. 567 F. Supp. 2d 1359 (N.D. Fla. 2008).
39. Ibid., 1363.
40. Ibid., 1364.
41. Ibid., 1375.
42. Ibid., 1370.
43. Ibid., at 1375.
44. Ibid., 1374 (internal citations and quotation marks omitted). The judge took the principal to task, writing, "Davis's conduct, in the capacity of a role model and authority figure is particularly deplorable in light of studies which confirm the vulnerability of gay and lesbian students." Ibid., 1370.
45. 445 F.3d 1166 (9th Cir. 2006).
46. The Gay Lesbian and Straight Education Network (GLSEN), in collaboration with the United States Student Association, sponsors the National Day of Silence each year. This student-focused event enables students to call attention to anti-LGBT (lesbian, gay, bisexual and transgendered) "name-calling, bullying, and harassment in schools" through their day-long vow of silence. Many students carry cards which read:

Please understand my reasons for not speaking today. I am participating in the Day of Silence, a national youth movement bringing attention to the silence faced by lesbian, gay, bisexual and transgender people and their allies in schools. My deliberate silence echoes that silence, which is caused by name-calling, bullying and harassment. I believe that ending the silence is the first step toward fighting these injustices. Think about the voices you are not hearing today. What are you going to do to end the silence? GLSEN, Day of Silence (2009), *at* http://www.dayofsilence.org/downloads/dos_speaking_card_09.pdf

In response to the National Day of Silence, the Alliance Defense Fund sponsors a counterprotest called "The Day of Truth." The Day of Truth "was established to counter the promotion of the homosexual agenda and express an opposing viewpoint from a Christian perspective." (ADF, ADF Day of Truth [2009], at http://www.dayoftruth.org/main/default.aspx.) During the Day of Truth, some students have chosen to express contrary views about supporting LGBT students. In a few cases, students have worn T-shirts to school condemning homosexuality.

47. Ibid., 1171.
48. Ibid.
49. Ibid., 1172.
50. Ibid., 1177, quoting Tinker v. Des Moines Independent Community School District, 393 U.S. 503, 508 (1969).
51. Ibid., 1178.
52. Ibid.
53. Ibid.
54. Ibid., 1179.
55. Ibid.
56. Ibid., 1183.
57. *See* Amanda L. Houle, "From T-Shirts to Teaching: May Public Schools Constitutionally Regulate Anti-Homosexual Speech? 76 *Fordham Law Review* 2477 (2008). "This Note further posits that *Harper* properly interpreted *Tinker*, and that schools may regulate anti-homosexual hate speech in the interests of protecting the rights of homosexual students." Ibid., 2503.
58. Ibid., 1178–79.
59. Ibid., 1179.
60. 145 F. Supp. 2d 1068 (D. Minn. 2001).
61. Ibid., 1070.
62. The court specifically rejected Elliott's argument that the school was promoting homosexuality. To the contrary, the court stated, "By displaying posters and lists of staff members who are willing to talk about issues of sexuality . . . , the school has made a conscious and commendable effort at creating an environment of tolerance and respect for diversity." Ibid., 1073.

63. Ibid., 1074.
64. Ibid., 1073.
65. Ibid.
66. 383 F. Supp. 2d 965 (S.D. Ohio 2005).
67. Ibid., 967.
68. Ibid., 968.
69. Ibid., 973.
70. Ibid.
71. Ibid., 966.
72. 636 F.3d 874 (7th Cir. 2011).
73. Nuxoll v. Indian Prairie School District, 523 F.3d 668, 676 (7th Cir. 2008).
74. Zamecnik v. Indian Prairie School District, 636 F.3d 874, 876 (7th. Cir. 2011).
75. Judge Kozinski asserted, "As Judge Gilman said in his persuasive dissent in *Boroff v. Van Wert City Board of Education*, 220 F.3d 465 (6th Cir. 2000), 'school officials are not free to decide that only one side of a topic is open for discussion because the other side is too repugnant or demoralizing to listen to.' . . . I couldn't have said it better." Harper v. Poway 445 F.3d 1166, 1194-95 1201 (9th Cir. 2006) (Kozinski, J. dissenting).
76. For example, the Maine Supreme Judicial court, in a split decision, held that a transgendered student's rights were violated when her school prohibited her from using the girl's restroom at school. Doe v. Regional School Unit 26, No. 12-582 (Me. Jan. 30, 2014).
77. Jeremiah R. Newhall, Sex-Based Dress Codes and Equal Protection in Public Schools, 12 *Appalachian Journal of Law* 209, 212 (2013).
78. McMillen v. Itawamba County School District, 702 F. Supp.2d 699 (N.D. Miss. 2010).
79. 579 F.3d 502 (5th Cir. 2009).
80. Ibid., 505.
81. Ibid., 506.
82. Ibid., 510.
83. 391 U.S. 367 (1968).
84. *Palmer*, 579 F.3d at 510.
85. Ibid.
86. Ibid.
87. Ibid., 511.
88. Ibid.
89. Ibid.
90. Ibid.
91. Ibid., 513.

SIX

Policy Implications for Dress Codes

Balancing Rights and Responsibilities

> Do not conceive that fine clothes make fine men any more than fine
> feathers make fine birds. A plain genteel dress is more admired and
> obtains more credit than lace and embroidery in the Eyes of the judi-
> cious and sensible.
> —George Washington, Letter to his nephew Bushrod Washington,
> January 17, 1783

Jurisprudence on students' free expression rights has traveled a long road
since the Supreme Court's *Tinker* decision in 1969. "Gone are the days
when the government could constitutionally regulate appearance without rhyme or reason."[1] The court's guiding principle, that students have
a constitutional right to engage in nondisruptive free speech, has been
invoked in support of student demands to wear earrings, bracelets with
messages, sagging pants, and T-shirts with lewd or disruptive messages
and to cross-dress for the prom.

Often these disputes have led to litigation, and the outcome of this
litigation has been mixed. As a result, dress code litigation tends to look
more like potpourri than a unified, articulated body of case law.

Indeed, federal courts have not always ruled consistently, even when
reviewing very similar cases. For example, one federal court ruled that
the phrase "I ♥ Boobies" was vulgar when displayed on a bracelet at
school;[2] while another court ruled that the phrase constituted social commentary and was not "plainly lewd," and therefore could not be categorically banned.[3] We also saw that two courts could not agree about whether a student has a First Amendment right to wear an anti-abortion T-shirt
to school. And courts are not in agreement about the constitutional right

of students to proclaim anti-homosexual messages on their clothing in the school environment.

Nevertheless, in spite of the lack of clarity in the decisions discussed in this book, school leaders can take comfort from this fact: Since the Supreme Court decided the *Tinker* case in 1969, no federal court has ruled that a school district is without constitutional authority to implement and enforce a reasonable student dress code. Even in the *Tinker* case itself, the Supreme Court emphasized that it was considering a dispute about a rule against students' wearing black armbands to protest the war in Vietnam; it was not ruling on the constitutionality of a neutral dress code.[4]

Although the courts have not ruled with absolute consistency in dress-code cases, their decisions suggest some guidelines for school leaders when they draft or enforce school dress codes for students. First, school authorities would be wise to draft a clear and comprehensive student dress code and make sure all students and their parents obtain a copy.

At a minimum, student-dress policies should prohibit student clothing that conveys messages that the Supreme Court has said are censorable in the school environment. In line with *Tinker*, a dress code should state that clothing that disrupts the school environment or interferes with the rights of other students may not be worn at school. Pursuant to the court's guidance in *Fraser*, a school's dress code should ban student messages on clothing that are lewd, vulgar, indecent, or sexually suggestive.[5] Dress codes should also prohibit student messages that promote or celebrate illegal drug use or the abusive or illegal use of alcohol. Clearly, the Supreme Court's decision in *Morse v. Frederick* would support such a rule.

Second, school authorities should not treat students differently based on students' views on a particular issue. Thus, if the school permits students to wear T-shirts endorsing a pro-choice stance on abortion, they should not prohibit other students from wearing T-shirts that proclaim a pro-life viewpoint. We are reminded of the *Tinker* court's admonition, "In our system, students may not be regarded as closed-circuit recipients of only that which the State chooses to communicate. They may not be confined to the expression of those sentiments that are officially approved."[6] Second, if students perceive that school officials discriminate against certain student viewpoints when enforcing a school dress code, they will certainly be resentful and more likely to bring a lawsuit claiming a violation of their First Amendment rights.

Third, when enforcing a school dress code, school administrators should treat students respectfully regarding their views on controversial issues, even if they find a particular student's views repugnant. Several of the cases reviewed in this book involved disputes between students with traditional Christian views on the topics of abortion and homosexuality—beliefs that are often disfavored in progressive school environments. Even if school leaders believe these students' expressions are inappropriate at school, educators should present a respectful demeanor when they confront students about arguably inappropriate clothing. Showing respect may not keep a disappointed student or parent from filing a lawsuit, but it conveys a professional attitude of tolerance and reasonableness that all of us as professional educators should wish to see modeled in our public schools.

We close this volume with some observations about the impact of student-dress litigation on schools and their educational mission. In our opinion, lawsuits brought by students who claim a constitutional and unilateral right to wear what they want to school do a disservice to students, schools, and society.

First, this litigation trivializes the Constitution and the role of the courts by asking judges to analyze petty disputes such as the case involving a student's right to wear sagging pants to school under principles adopted in the *Tinker* decision, a case involving serious political speech. In our view, not all student conduct within the schoolhouse gate is entitled to the full panoply of constitutional protection.

After all, the school is a special place that is devoted to learning, and school authorities should be entitled to make reasonable decisions designed to maintain and enhance the school's learning atmosphere. Crop tops and pajama bottoms that might be tolerated in a public shopping mall need not be permitted in a high-school classroom. Bawdy quips and messages celebrating illegal drugs may be acceptable on the public boardwalks of our beaches but our public school hallways are another matter. As cogently expressed by Judge Newman, "the First Amendment gives a high school student the classroom right to wear Tinker's armband, but not Cohen's ["Fuck the draft"] jacket."[7]

Second, litigation over student dress codes may have the effect of discouraging local educators from making the commonsense decisions the public expects them to make concerning children's welfare. Whether a lawsuit has merit or not, the possibility of a civil rights suit over a dress-code provision may intimidate school administrators from adopting regulations designed to maintain a safe and orderly learning environment. For example, how eager will South Hadley school authorities be to adopt a new student-conduct regulation, having experienced protracted litigation over their efforts to ban "Coed Naked" T-shirts?[8]

Third, dress-code litigation subverts a primary mission of public education, which is to instill a decent respect for community values and civil speech.[9] That mission, the Supreme Court instructed in the *Fraser* decision, includes the duty to inculcate civic values and promote civil discourse. Students and their parents who disagree with the wording of a dress code are free to lobby the school board to change school policy. This is consistent with the procedures used to resolve other school disputes, such as disagreements about curricular decisions or school boards' decisions about allocating financial resources.

schools should not censor student speech on significant social issues simply because school authorities disfavor par-oints. But students and their families should not go to court disagree with school authorities about the appropriateness of a slogan that a student wishes to proclaim on a T-shirt. What message do children learn about civic responsibility when their parents bring lawsuits claiming that their family's preferences for sagging pants, lewd T-shirts, or clothes that make their children feel good are entitled to the same constitutional scrutiny that the Tinker children received when they protested, with courage and dignity, the Vietnam War?

Students have constitutional rights, such as the right to free speech, which public school educators are charged with protecting. Those rights must be respected, of course. However, we believe that a student's right to free speech must be balanced by a school's reasonable regulations designed to promote a safe and orderly learning environment for all students. After all, school administrators, not the courts, are best situated to determine whether a particular item of student clothing is vulgar or potentially disruptive.[10] Only decisions by administrators that punish speech that school authorities personally disagree with and that are not tied to a reasonable standard, such as a legitimate pedagogical concern,[11] should give rise to judicial intervention.

In addition to promoting an orderly school environment, reasonable school dress codes define boundaries of appropriateness that students will likely encounter in the work world. Of course it is appropriate to give students some latitude about their clothing choices, just as adults generally have some discretion about what they wear to work. Nevertheless, the classroom is a work environment for students and educators. To expect that students and educators wear clothing that reflects the importance of that work environment is not unreasonable.

We are not arguing that school officials should be free to act arbitrarily or capriciously when making decisions about students' attire. Reasonableness should be the touchstone for administrative decisions regarding student dress. And school officials should not be given the right to promote their own views on social issues while censoring students with opposing points of view. Rather, school authorities' decisions about student dress should be motivated by the desire to maintain a school environment conducive for learning for all students.

The Supreme Court would be performing a valuable service for public education if it articulated a clear standard for determining students' right to choose their school attire. Until it does so, the federal courts are likely to continue ruling inconsistently in student dress-code cases, which will discourage school officials from enforcing reasonable dress codes out of fear of being sued.

"Our decision to implement an interim revised dress policy . . . was made to avoid the certain continued time, unreasonable expense and disruption to our primary mission of educating students that this litigation ensures."

John Glaser, Superintendent, Napa [Valley Unified] School District on [the] decision to settle, rather than fight, a lawsuit about the district's dress code.*

Citizens Against Lawsuit Abuse, "The Fourth 'R' of California's School District: 'Ripped off by Litigation'" (January 2008), p. 7, available at http://www.cala.com/docs/schoolsreport.pdf.

In an earlier chapter, we discussed *Palmer v. Waxahachie Independent School District*, in which the Fifth Circuit analyzed a Texas school district's dress code similar to the way federal courts have analyzed school-uniform policies. The Waxahachie policy prohibited all messages on students' clothing, except the school logo or messages that promoted school spirit and were approved by the principal.[12] The Fifth Circuit concluded that this restrictive dress code was content neutral and treated all clothing-borne messages the same without regard to their content. Moreover, the court concluded that the school district had a valid governmental interest in implementing its dress code and that the code restricted student speech no more than was necessary to fulfill the school's governmental interest.

In its *Waxahachie* opinion, the Fifth Circuit observed that the school district's clothing restrictions were not onerous. Students could still wear what they wished outside the school day. Moreover, there were other avenues of expression for students besides proclaiming messages on their clothing. Thus, a viewpoint-neutral rule banning all messages on clothing except those pertaining to school spirit was not unreasonable.

We think the Fifth Circuit's ruling in the *Waxahachie* case offers a clearer guideline for determining the constitutionality of student dress codes than the current legal framework, which permits federal courts to determine on a case-by-case basis whether a school district can ban a particular item of student clothing based on its potential for disruptiveness or a court's subjective view as to whether the student's clothing is vulgar.

Frankly, schools and students would be better served by a constitutional rule that permits schools to ban all messages on student clothing and to insist on reasonable rules for modesty and decorum than they are by the current legal landscape, which allows students and their parents to claim constitutional protection for the clothing they wear to school. Students who wish to speak on controversial issues should be encouraged to do so in the student newspaper, in student clubs, during oral conversations at appropriate times, and in after-school activities. But the right of school authorities to enforce reasonable dress codes, including the right to ban messages on students' clothing, should be consistently upheld by the courts.

NOTES

1. Jennifer L. Greenblat, "Using the Equal Protection Clause Post-VMI to Keep Gender Stereotypes Out of the Public School Dress Code Equation," 13 *UC Davis Journal of Juvenile Law & Policy* 281, 282 (2009).

2. J.A. v. Fort Wayne Community Schools, 2013 U.S. Dist. LEXIS 117667 (N.D. Ind. 2013).

3. B.H. v. Easton Area School District, 725 F.3d 293 (3d Cir. 2013).

4. Tinker v. Des Moines Independent Community School District, 393 U.S. 503, 507–8 (1969) ("The problem posed by the present case does not relate to regulation of the length of skirts or the type of clothing, to hair style, or deportment.").

5. The judge in Pyle v. South Hadley School Committee, 861 F. Supp. 150, 170 (D. Mass. 1994) wrote that school dress codes can protect students from "an environment of unrelenting winks, snickering, and sexual prodding."

6. Ibid. at 509.

7. *Thomas v. Board of Education, Granville Central School District*, 607 F.2d 1043, 1057 (2nd Cir. 1979) (Judge Newman's concurring opinion).

8. Legal expenses in the *Pyle* litigation totaled around $30,000, according to Norman Guertin, administrative assistant to the Board of Selectmen. William A. Davis. 1996. "When the Shirt Hits the Fan." *The Boston Globe* (January 10) 25, 28, p. 28.

9. Bethel School District v. Fraser, 478 U.S. 675 (1986).

10. For example, a federal district court in Nebraska supported the school administrators' ban on a T-shirt based on their evidence that it would cause a substantial disruption. The T-shirt had the initials "R.I.P." memorializing a student (Julius Robinson), a gang member who was allegedly killed by members of a rival gang, the Omaha Mafia Bloods. Kuhr v. Millard Public School District, No. 8:09CV363 (April 23, 2012), p. 2. Available at http://www.splc.org/pdf/kuhr_dverdict.pdf .

11. Hazelwood School District v. Kuhlmeier, 484 U.S. 260 (1988).

12. Palmer v. Waxahachie Independent School District, 579 F.3d 502 (5th Cir. 2009).

Index

About the Authors

Richard Fossey (B.A., Oklahoma State University; M.A. University of Texas at Austin; J.D., University of Texas School of Law at Austin; Ed.D., Harvard University) is the Paul Burdin Endowed Professor of Education at the University of Louisiana at Lafayette. Previously, he was professor and Mike Moses Endowed Chair in Educational Leadership at the University of North Texas. Prior to joining the academy, he practiced law in Alaska for nine years, where he represented school districts in Alaska Native communities.

He served on the board of directors of the Education Law Association from 2004 to 2007. He is editor of *Catholic Southwest* and serves on the editorial advisory committee of *West's Education Law Reporter*. He has written numerous articles and book chapters on education law and policy. His books include *Crime on Campus: Legal Issues and Campus Administration* (co-authored with Michael C. Smith), *Condemning Students to Debt: College Loans and Public Policy* (co-edited with Mark Bateman), *Sexual Orientation, Public Schools, and the Law* (co-authored with Todd A. DeMitchell and Suzanne Eckes), and *Contemporary Issues in Higher Education Law* (co-edited with Kerry B. Melear and Joseph C. Beckham).

Todd A. DeMitchell (B.A., La Verne College; M.A.T., University of La Verne; M.A., University of California at Davis; Ed.D., University of Southern California; Post-Doctorate, Harvard University) spent eighteen years in the public schools in California serving as a substitute teacher, elementary school teacher, assistant principal (K–6), principal (K–8), director of personnel and labor relations (K–12), and superintendent (K–8). Currently, he is a professor in the Education Department and the Justice Studies Program at the University of New Hampshire. In addition, he is the chair of the faculty senate for the university. He has served as associate chair and chair of the Education Department. He was designated Distinguished Professor by the University of New Hampshire. In addition, he received a teaching excellence award, was named Kimball Faculty Fellow in education and Lamberton Professor of Justice Studies, and he received a research award from the New England Educational Research Organization.

His research focuses on school law and labor relations. This is his sixth book and his fourth book with Rowman & Littlefield Education. His previous books with Rowman & Littlefield include The *Limits of Law-*

Based School Reform: Vain Hopes and False Promises (co–authored with Richard Fossey), *Negligence: What Principals Need to Know about Avoiding Liability,* and *Labor Relations in Education: Policies, Politics, and Practices.* He has published over 150 law review articles, book chapters, peer reviewed journal articles, and commentaries. His publications have appeared in such journals as *Southern California Interdisciplinary Law Journal; Journal of College and University Law; Connecticut Public Interest Law Journal; Cardozo Public Law, Policy, and Ethics Journal; Boston University Public Interest Law Journal; Education and Law Journal; Brigham Young University Education and Law Journal;* and the *Journal of Law & Education.*

Made in the USA
San Bernardino, CA
05 June 2018